Writing Family History
Made Very Easy

By the same author:

Remembering Mothers: An inspiring anthology of short stories, letters and poetry, (eds) N. Kyle, L. Semple and J. Gracie Mulcahy

Memories & Dreams: A Biography of Nurse Mary Kirkpatrick

A Class of its Own: A History of Queensland University of Technology, with Joanne Scott and Catherine Manathunga

The Family History Writing Book, with Ron King

We Should've Listened to Grandma: Women and Family History

Her Natural Destiny: The Education of Women in New South Wales

Tracing Family History in Australia

Writing Family History Made Very Easy

Noeline Kyle

ALLEN&UNWIN

Allen & Unwin
83 Alexander Street
Crows Nest NSW 2065
Australia
Phone: (61 2) 8425 0100
Fax: (61 2) 9906 2218
Email: info@allenandunwin.com
Web: www.allenandunwin.com

National Library of Australia
Cataloguing-in-Publication entry:

Kyle, Noeline.
   Writing family history made very easy: a beginner's guide.

   Bibliography.
   Includes index.
   ISBN 978 1 74175 062 1.

   1. Genealogy—Authorship. 2. Genealogy—Handbooks, manuals, etc. I. Title.

929.1

Set in 11/16 pt Sabon by Bookhouse, Sydney
Printed and bound in Australia by Griffin Press

10 9 8 7 6 5 4 3 2

CONTENTS

PREFACE

Writing Family History Made Very Easy has emerged out of my years of teaching writing to family historians. Over the last decade I have facilitated family history writing groups and have taught lively students who have brought with them a diverse range of writing approaches. I have learned much from these students of life, writing and family history, and am grateful for their wisdom, their generosity of spirit and their willingness to share.

There is no doubt we find writing more difficult than we do the research task. Students have told me time and again about their frustrations with a writing and publishing process in family history that seems overwhelming to them.

This book is written to help family historians to write and write well. It is not possible, of course, to teach anyone to write overnight or indeed to do so in a few weeks. Learning to write is a process. Learning to write family history will take time.

What this book can do, however, is provide practical and useful strategies so that you can begin writing, so that you will continue writing, and to enable you to plan and publish a professional family history. And, the best thing you can do as a writer, or as a potential writer, is to sit down and write.

This book provides practical advice, useful information, and strategies drawn from my many years of working with family historians as well as my expertise as a professional historian. This book is aimed at getting you to the desk and writing. And once you are writing, this book will take you systematically through the writing, editing and publishing process so that you will be able to write and publish your book.

I am grateful for, and have benefited greatly from, my interaction with many individuals and organisations in family history. Over the years I have worked with, and drawn on the expertise of, members associated with the Newcastle Family History Society, Illawarra Family History Group, Queensland Family History Society, Society of Australian Genealogists, Richmond Tweed Family History Society, Northern Rivers Family History Writers' Group, Byron Bay Writers' Centre and New South Wales Writers' Centre.

I have talked to many enthusiastic family historians who have shared with me their stories, their successes and their failures during their research and writing experiences. I thank them all, and am grateful for the valuable and generous insights they have shared with me.

I want to thank Dawn Montgomery, Robert Adamson, Ann West, Annette Baxter, Elaine Pollard, Sue Reid, Terry

Garvey and Ellen MacDonald who shared their writing of family history with me in the mid 1990s as members of the Queensland Family History Society Writers' Interest Group. I need to thank Tanya Binning, Jill Richards Brennan, Lois Carroll, Deirdre Cox, Yvonne Hammond, Hazel Holmes, Jan Gracie Mulcahy, Lybbie Semple and Barbara Worthington for four wonderful years of membership of the Northern Rivers Family History Writers' Group. These men and women have taught me humility and tolerance for difference and diversity in writing as well as much, much more about the richness and uniqueness of individual storytelling in family history.

Finally, I would like to thank my publisher Annette Barlow for her encouragement and support, and my editor Catherine Taylor for her patience and meticulous editing of this work. I, of course, take responsibility for the final text. I dedicate it to my mother and thank her for taking responsibility for the family that nurtured me all of my life.

Noeline Kyle, 2006

Chapter one ᚺ

WRITING IS A
LEARNED SKILL

W**ould you like to begin writing, now?
Would you like to learn quickly and
have fun writing? Then, read on...**

Lesson one! Writing is a learned skill

We grow up with two myths about writing; the first is a belief
that successful writers are born to write. The second myth
we hold is that we cannot learn to write.

Let's begin this lesson on writing family history more easily
by throwing these two myths into the wastepaper basket!

Anyone can learn to write. Not everyone will be a best-
selling author. However, every writer can learn to write well
and improve their writing by following a few easy steps. This
book aims to introduce a range of easy strategies and ideas
for you to do just that.

Firstly, the book will show you how writing can be learned easily and well. Secondly, it will provide simple, straightforward advice for writing and publishing a well-planned, well-written family history.

As a family historian, you have completed careful and detailed research already. Draw on this to begin your writing of the family history. Family historians use genealogical software to store and record their family names, dates and various family relationships. This, too, provides a solid foundation for beginning writing.

You have a pedigree chart finished? Good. Use it. The meticulous research work required to compile your charts is a perfect stepping-off point for your first drafts.

Study closely the range of information contained in certificates, obituaries, letters, census entries, books, press cuttings and photocopied articles, and listen carefully to collected oral histories. This initial reading and listening are the basic building blocks for beginning writing.

Birth certificates will have place names, and the names of midwives or doctors for you to puzzle over and link to stories. From this basic data you can begin sketching a picture of how and where the birth occurred. You can think about time and the seasons; whether it was winter or summer and how this might have affected the family for a birth, death or marriage event. You can determine from your reading just how old other children were at the time of a birth and if the father was at home or away at work.

A close reading of your documents, examining the names, relationships and how these link to or affect each other, can provide entry points for your writing. You can then plunge headlong into the exciting world of shaping your family story, and add the historical depth and the splashes of writing colour that every good story needs.

Lesson two! Writing is fun

Learning to write family history well requires curiosity, wisdom, personal dedication, self-confidence, planning, thinking strategies, emotional strength, good notetaking, organisation, interpretation, imagination, creativity, ideas, resources, editing skills, good writing friends AND A SENSE OF HUMOUR!

Having read most of the books currently available on writing, publishing and editing, I have benefited greatly from the advice of others. But, some authors are too ready to lecture the beginning writer, and their advice can be confusing and difficult to understand!

There is not much fun or clarity in advice such as '...the most evocative words create visceral or kinesthetic images...' or '...the traditional well-made plot is an artificial thing...' If the beginning writer is looking for easy-to-follow or practical pathways to their writing, it is not found in this advice. Nor will they find much fun!

Writing should be a joyful, creative, enthralling experience. Over the last ten years I have led several family history writing groups, and their main aim was to improve writing skills but not, I add, at the expense of having fun.

Good writing has an emotional core; it has passion and verve; it has irony and wry humour, and it helps to be able to laugh at yourself. It is also useful to step back from your writing, pause and reflect on the process. Remind yourself that this is just the beginning. In other words, enjoy the journey. In the end, writing is about the journey, the processes and the experiences of you as the writer, as much as it is about the text. You are learning to be a writer and a historian. As you craft your stories, new windows into thinking about family history will emerge and you, too, will change as a researcher, writer and historian.

To write good history there is no doubt you require all of the technical, language and creative skills you can muster. And you need passion, compassion and a sense of humour. Tanya Binning, in her oral history of Iris Perkins, has written the following compassionate and entertaining piece:

Running down our steep driveway Mum would call out, 'Don't fall over and dirty your white stockings!' I was so proud of myself, taking off down our dirt road all by myself going to our Bush Mission Sunday School. If I am asked my religion today, I say Bush Mission! During our service, we were taught kindness towards people and how to look after them and that helped me at home. Johnny walked with me some Sundays, I liked that because I could talk to him and he always protected me. Our preacher's wife, Mrs Ashman, gave out clothes to all the children who had walked there. We were a varied race of Chinese, Italian, Aboriginal as well as us Anglo Bushies and we were all treated equally.[1]

With family history writing, you are lucky to have a strong emotional link to the research and writing. These provide a unique source of inspiration and energy to begin, and then continue with, the writing task.

And, once you relax, see writing as fun, and link in to what others are writing about, you can build a shared space for writing, a sense of purpose and direction, and gain self-confidence to improve and ease the writing task.

Who's writing this story?

I tell my students to write quickly at first without thinking too much about sentence structure or style.

Do not worry at first about the exaggerated phrases, the wild generalisations, the turgid sentences, the disparate thoughts or the uncoordinated ideas that seem to flow so easily from

the pen! Read this turgid long sentence from *Memories &*
Dreams:

Still, her memories of childhood were dominated by her
parent's (sic) unending struggle, their battle with harsh,
economic and social conditions; the unending struggle of
her mother's working life in the linen factory, the struggle
of hard labour for men like her father in the rope factory
and the struggle to keep clean and respectable in the filthy,
flooded and neglected dock area of Bridge End,
Ballymacarrett.[2]

I am breathless now reading this sentence! It is long and
repetitious. Given the chance I could rewrite as follows:

Her memories of childhood were dominated by poverty and
hard times. Her parents were factory workers, their lives
dominated by harsh economic and social conditions. There
was, too, the struggle to keep clean and respectable in the
filthy, flooded and neglected dock area of Bridge End,
Ballymacarrett.

However, this is the beginning phase of finding *your voice*.
You need to get the ideas, the stories and the passion onto
the page. If the sentences are too long at first or there is
unnecessary repetition, no matter for now. You can worry
about fixing the sentences, and the syntax, later.

Often our first drafts are stilted or clichéd and overwritten. Do not be discouraged. Keep on writing and rewriting. Your *writing voice* will develop that tone, that style, that turn of phrase, that will eventually delight you. It will feel comfortable. It does not have to be perfect. But it is your voice, it is how you will write about your family, and it will, in the end, be unique to you.

A family history can be written in any genre including fiction. Memoir and biographical approaches have become increasingly popular with family historians as they search for new and creative ways of telling family and personal histories.

Most family history will fit within what might be called an interpretive genre. You gather together all of the 'facts' and then interpret them. You make an assessment of how ancestors coped during economic depressions, what they did at work, how they responded to world wars or as settlers in a new country. You reflect on family relationships, family conflict, and the grief, joy and hope that people experienced each day of their lives.

There is no right way to write a family history. There is no specific genre that is best. If you prefer a traditional approach, that is fine. It is equally acceptable to write from your imagination or perhaps choose an approach somewhere between the two.

If you have difficulty thinking of what to write or how to write about a complex event or relationship, try to re-phrase your words and ideas in basic prose. Think about what it is you want to write, and use words that convey your meaning as clearly as possible. Keep your writing specific and straightforward. Use active words and write as you would talk.

I have found that some beginning writers take to dialogue very quickly. They have a good ear for the language of their childhood, and they can remember family conversations seemingly word for word. Other beginners prefer to write a traditional family history. They like a beginning, a middle and an end.

In some cases beginning writers value the emotional connection they feel for their stories and the characters. Their personal journey with the writing process is an integral part of the writing and the family history.

But whatever genre or voice you use for your family history, ensure the reader understands what is 'true' and what is not. It is a simple matter to say 'I imagine that my grandmother said' or 'Uncle Arthur remembered that'. Or to write a preface informing readers that the dialogue in the book is based on stories told in the family and passed down through the generations and are not necessarily 'true'.

Personally speaking

Each of us has a view about family, politics, history and world events. Some of us are more forceful than others about them.

Nonetheless, stated or not, everyone has prejudice and bias in their thinking about the world. As writers we need to understand our bias and prejudices, if our writing is to be credible and professional.

When I wrote my family history, my main readers were family but I wanted to broaden the appeal of the story to others by locating it in a broader context, that is, beyond the family. The local history I included in my research and writing was useful for the family but had an appeal beyond this as well. An emphasis on women ancestors was also a broader theme in the book.

My training as a professional historian and my interest in women's history led me to take the approach that I did, and shaped how I eventually wrote the family history. I had, too, a personal interest in how single mothers survived in Australian history as my mother and my great grandmother were single parents; my great grandmother in the 1890s, and my mother in the 1950s.

These personal experiences, together with a professional interest in women's history, were influential in shaping how my family history was finally written. How you choose the approach for your writing will be different, but there will be reasons, ideas and family or personal experiences that inform your choice.

Our belief systems about the family or the roles of men and women, about religion, marriage and parenthood, about ethnicity, war, the environment, government, work, single parents, senior citizens and disability, are topics that engage us almost daily. And we have a view about them, even if we do not stand up and say so.

You will write more convincing family history if you check what other views are held on particular issues in history.

Writing history is not everything in the past

One of the most common questions I am asked by family historians is how to fill in research gaps to write a 'complete' family history.

This question is linked to a research gap that someone has found of around ten or fifteen years and the frustration of not being able to find any records or family event to fill it.

These research gaps are often found when immigrants or convicts first arrive in Australia. The family live for a time in Sydney and five or ten years later they emerge in another place, perhaps in a country town or in another state.

Our only tracking device for the family during this time are the births or deaths of family members, but there is little surviving in the records to tell us about how the family lived and worked out their daily lives.

This is a universal problem for all history, not just for family history. Professional and amateur historians spend a great deal of their time in dusty archives reading tightly written pages that are smudged and worn with age—in fact barely readable! They try desperately to find as many of these as possible in an effort to build more accurate and complete pictures of the past. Nevertheless they are rarely able to fill in every gap.

It is not possible to find everything and nor is it possible to know everything about the past. History writing is not everything that happened in the past but the part of it that you decide is significant for your own family stories.

As you research and write, you will gain insights into the long past and, with some imagination and judicious interpretation, be able to fill in some gaps. But finding gaps and uncertainty in your research should not stop you writing easily and well.

So relax! Filling in the gaps in your family story can lead you into more imaginative writing territory, different and exciting approaches, and, in the end, easier and more professional writing.

Focus and planning

I used an individual, my great grandmother, as the central character to my family history. This provided a strategy or focus to keep my story on track. I could still write the stories of my family but within a more planned writing frame that gave the story coherence, clarity and a point of view.

In the nineteenth and twentieth centuries, officials of the state wrote Australian history. The resultant history was less critical of ruling governments and dominant groups. Minority groups, women, children, the working classes and everyday life were ignored. This is not to say that such histories were 'wrong'. But they were one-sided and biased.

Family history, in many ways, is the opposite of these early histories—we are filling in the spaces left by official history. We are writing the family stories that connect us to a richer, more diverse and challenging past. Choosing a focus—such as a character, an event or an occupation—is one way of keeping your writing on track.

Example

In the following piece, 'Cradle to the Grave', Yvonne Hammond is writing about the birth of her mother in January 1890. The descriptive and emotional text setting the scene is a compelling, poignant and amusing story of her mother:

In tight formation the houses marched up St Michaels Hill, shoulder to shoulder, supporting each other against the mist, as it played its nightly game. Swirling and cavorting in ever darkening shadows, seeking an entry, to creep and touch with icy fingers everything within the walls. Tonight the mist, dark and foreboding, was a portend maybe, of the life and death struggle occurring in number ninety one, where young Rachel, my grandmother, was in dire trouble! . . .

Drifting in and out of consciousness, dark, unnatural dreams suffused her mind, despairing of death. Calling occasionally 'Come and help me Mother, PLEASE, Mother, please.' The midwife, giving some encouragement, says in a soothing voice 'Just bear down there's a good girl; it will all be over soon,' in silent prayer, hoping her assumption is correct . . .

Hour after painful hour dragged on, the shuddering spasms continued, but as the first grey fingers of daylight penetrated the room, also came realisation—at last—the birth was imminent. 'Thank you God' said the midwife. With a final extreme effort, my grandmother delivered the tiny infant safely into the tired grateful hands of the midwife, as the visiting *Shadow of death* departed.

Grandmother Rachel pressed my mother close to her breast in joyful amazement. So happy was she with the knowledge, that the dark visitor, who had loomed so ominously for many hours, was unceremoniously banished with the triumph of this new birth. Who could foretell that the struggled entry of this babe into the world on 1 January 1890 would set a pattern for the rest of her life?[3]

Written by an 83-year-old woman as part of a project writing about mothers and mothering, this story has a strong imaginative framework. Yvonne Hammond's telling of family stories has continued in this creative way, using dialogue and re-creating the conversations of her childhood and youth with a lightness, deftness and skill rarely found in most family history.

EXERCISES

Memory ensures that things do not just happen and then disappear without a trace. Memory is selective and unreliable, but it is the one powerful strategy you have to reconstruct, retrieve and write significant parts of the family history.

* A sense of place deepens your understanding of the past. If possible, travel to and become familiar again with the house/s, the land and the specific characteristics of the place/s you are writing about. Look at the landscape and imagine your ancestors living and working within it.

* Write down what you see (including what you imagine), how you feel, and the emotional and the historical connections you draw from this visit and their impact on your present.

* Begin a style sheet to keep track of various names (and spellings of names), names of places and institutions, hyphenated words, abbreviations, dates, capitalisations, numbers, punctuation, initials, nicknames and important terms. Keep a good dictionary and thesaurus open as you write and revise your writing. Do not rely on the spellchecker or the language thesaurus in your word-processing program.

Getting started

Do not limit how you will write your family history. Read this extract from *Wild Swans* and write a short piece of similar length based on your own experience or from a story told to you by your parents or grandparents, or perhaps 'imagined' from the previous exercise:

> My grandmother's feet had been bound when she was two years old. Her mother, who herself had bound feet, first wound a piece of white cloth about twenty feet long round her feet, bending all the toes except the big toe inward and under the sole. Then she placed a large stone on top to crush the arch. My grandmother screamed in agony and begged her to stop. Her mother had to stick a clot into her mouth to gag her. My grandmother passed out repeatedly from the pain.[4]

It is a time to be creative with your writing. It is not the final draft. It is a beginning, it is a way into writing, and it is here you will begin to understand that such stories can ease you into creative and challenging writing if you relax, have fun, see the bigger picture and stay true to your story.

Chapter two ❧

BECOMING A WRITER

Too much expert advice? Feeling confused?
Then throw away the books and conquer
those barriers you keep finding to writing
easily and well.

Too much expert advice

If there is a syndrome, here it is—the 'too much expert advice'
syndrome!

You read or listen to so much advice about what not to
do in writing history that you are overwhelmed and cannot
write. You believe the myths of how you are not a real writer
or that writing history is only for the professionals. And frozen
in this negative state, you give up.

Why not challenge this negative state. Why not think of
ourselves as researchers *and writers* and, indeed, as confident

family historians. Let me begin this chapter with some questions that aim to encourage you to think of yourself as a writer, too.

Are you a family historian?

Are you a parent? Are you a grandparent? Are you a worker? Are you a family historian? Are you a researcher? Yes, I hear you say.

There is no doubt that we think of ourselves as family historians. In addition, our research task continues to stretch tantalisingly in front of us the best and most compelling thing to happen to us in decades.

Are you a writer? A more tentative answer. Yes? No? Why is it that we put up a barrier to thinking of ourselves as writers of family history despite spending months and years completing the research and writing task? Why is it that you do not see yourself so easily as a writer when you so enthusiastically, and quite rightly, view yourself as a competent and confident researcher?

You become an expert very quickly with research. As a family historian, you learn the intricate nature of the particular research you embark on, including the complexity of library and archival cataloguing. You are absorbed in, and very soon expert on, the detail and the diversity of your original ancestry whether from Ireland, England, Scotland, Wales, Germany, France, Sweden, South America, India, China or the Middle East.

Visit the monthly meetings of any family history group and members can tell you with little effort what research they are doing, where they intend to research next, and how important and interesting these activities are to them.

However, you place writing as an activity apart from the research. You look at the writing task with dismay—too late! Too late, you might think, to have a better grasp on how to organise this large and growing research task into a professional and easily managed writing job.

It is never too late. Look up from your research task, take a deep breath and begin to think of yourself as a writer, too.

Think of yourself as a writer

You do not have to be a best-selling author to be a writer. You are a writer if you work on business reports or help complete drafts of text for community organisations. You are a writer when you compile that agenda with its innumerable lengthy attachments. You are a writer when you write in a daily journal or diary.

You do not have to be published to be a writer. The literary concept of a writer is elitist. It can exclude those of us who put pen to paper for the first time or who do not aspire to be the next Tolstoy or J.K. Rowling.

Writing is a term that can be applied to the tiniest piece of text such as a short note or letter. Family historians can be competent, even brilliant writers. The possibilities for you as a writer are endless so long as writing is a place you want to be.

Enjoy the writing

Be confident about your writing. You can be a beginner or an experienced writer. You can write drafts, rewrite and change your text, and still be a writer. You can write parts of a family history and leave it for months, years, and still be a writer.

Becoming a writer is a journey and each step along the way will encourage you to think more positively, about who you are.

When I first started to write in earnest, I was in my mid 30s and enrolled as a student at a TAFE college. With great trepidation I wrote my first English essay, a mere half-page. The teacher handed it back and rather kindly, I thought, told me it was a good start but could I make it longer next time!

It took many years for me to understand fully the writing process. It was an introduction to Australian history, and then my participation in family history and women's history, which provided the inspiration, the enthusiasm and the creativity to write those longer pieces.

As you write longer drafts of your family history, connect them to other stories and link into other histories—you will be a more confident writer, too. Research, writing and history-making are your entry into an exhilarating, creative voyage of self-discovery.

There is always another story

Some family historians tell me that when they have finished their family history they will never write again. They see the task of writing as a finite thing. It will be over soon, almost like a dentist's visit! But is this really so?

The writing of one part of the family history often leads to a desire to write a more specific story such as a biography, memoir or autobiography.

You begin the research journey believing, perhaps, that there is an end point for it. Perhaps you begin with the idea that you will find that elusive first ancestor in Ireland, England, Scotland, Italy, Russia, Brazil, Canada or Turkey—and there, you say, it is finished!

You have a clean line of research stretching from your mother or father and leading to neat, simple origins. In addition, when you have collected, recorded and filed these connecting names, dates and relationships, that will be the end of it. The generations will fall neatly into place and the family lineage will be complete.

It soon becomes clear, however, that family history research and writing is not like this at all. In the end, there is not one line stretching back to an original ancestor but many trees and numerous branches. It is a choice you make—to write your story from the many versions of 'what happened' in your past.

I chose to write about my mother's family. I had listened to many stories about the Irish origins of my great grandmother, and her life and career as a midwife became the focus of my research. That line is traced through my mother's paternal grandmother but there are many other lines of research I could have taken. My mother's maternal grandmother's family were English, my father's origins are Irish and Scottish. I have convicts, free settlers, soldiers, midwives and farmers waiting in the past to be retrieved for family history.

The writing of family history can focus on one line, or it can be about one person, or it can be a mix of many branches. As the creator of the family history, you choose which story you want to focus on, which tree or branch to investigate, and then write about.

By choosing one story, however, you leave out others, perhaps to research and mull over later. There is always another story.

In the end, each of us will understand that writing family history is an imperfect, incomplete and ever-changing task. The greatest discovery for the family historian is the knowledge that they can return time and again to write many stories and many family histories.

Mythical beliefs

Myth 1: Belief that we cannot write

Perhaps the biggest barrier to writing is a belief that you cannot write. Writing, you think, is a talent other people have and the rest of us are mere plodders who cannot take part. This is a myth.

Writing your family history is nothing like the writing you did at school. Unlike the forced compositions of your schooldays, writing stories about your family is something you want to do. Your aim is to write a family history that your family will read and enjoy.

That writing task is well within your grasp if you prepare well, think systematically about it and plan your writing beforehand. It will help, too, if you view the writing of your family history as being equally as important as the researching of it.

Myth 2: Belief that we do not have time to write

This belief relates to busy lives. How many times have you said that you do not have time to plan and then write the family history? Perhaps you have also said that you will have more time when you retire, or when the children leave home. You will wait, you think, until there are fewer family or work commitments in your life.

It is true that work and family will always need your

attention. But writing is a task that requires some discipline and commitment, and it can be done irrespective of other aspects of your life.

Our minds are cluttered with the other demands that are made upon us as parents, workers, grandparents and community participants. They will always be there.

Either you want to do it or you do not. Yes, it is difficult to make space for writing. But, if you want to write then set aside the time each day for it. This may take some negotiating with other family or friends at first as you establish your right to make time for this task.

Myth 3: Belief that we will appear foolish

No one likes to trip up in public. There is little doubt that writing reveals parts of us we might have wanted kept secret. Publishing a list of names and dates is not particularly revealing, of course, and if that is all you do then this advice is not particularly relevant.

But if you write family history where you describe characters, imagine feelings, examine motives and interpret significant family events and relationships, you will be writing, in part, from the self and in the text reveal aspects of your own hopes, desires and fears to the reader.

One way to temper these fears is to share your writing drafts and your writing ideas with other family members and fellow historians. Sharing your thoughts and ideas and then writing about the family should help calm these fears.

Myth 4: *Belief that writing is a one-off activity*

Few of us can sit down once only and write a final draft. It is a myth to think that the shaping of your family stories will be done in a single draft on that day you decide for it to happen. Good writing is not a one-off activity.

On the contrary, the writing, rewriting, re-reading, re-shaping and revising will be done many times, and at a diverse number of points, along the way of your writing journey. Occasionally parts of the text emerge more easily, but the writing task is a journey or a progression along a logical and disciplined path.

Writing history requires discipline, commitment, energy and a real desire to do it. It requires you to sit down every day and sift through, not just your previous research, but your writing and its relationship to the bigger stories in your head. There will be a long period of months, indeed years, to completion.

However, you do not have to give up other parts of your life to do it. You can write part-time, and you can move in and out of your research and writing over many years. The way you do manage your writing time is up to you.

How to conquer the barriers

You will be surprised how easy it is to overcome barriers to writing, and writing well. Following are some successful strategies to get you started and to ease the writing process.

Beginning writing is timid

Beginning writing is rarely confident. As you gather new ideas and information from your research, your writing will change. New insights and different interpretations will emerge and your writing will gain in clarity, confidence and professionalism as you become more familiar with it.

Rewriting is not editing

Revising and rewriting your many drafts will bring ideas and concepts, that is, your draft writing, toward a more concise, clearer and more fluid expression of your family history.

However, it is not editing. You should not be searching for grammatical or spelling errors too obsessively at first. Correct errors if you find them, but leave close editing until you have completed final drafts. The purpose of early revision is to clarify your writing and to bring together disparate and disconnected prose into a more integrated whole. Leave critical editing to later, more finished text.

Read, read, read

Reading widely—fiction, biography, news stories, bulletins, magazines, history, popular non-fiction—is a powerful adjunct to the writing process.

Good writers read widely and they read with a critical eye on how other writers use language, compose paragraphs,

25

develop characters, tell stories and anecdotes, and draw on the past and the present for their stories.

Examine how other writers look at and explore family relationships? How do they begin the story, shape the content and then work toward a conclusion? How do other writers understand and write about family and work, the role of women and children, family conflict, immigration, and the many other themes and ideas that you want to examine in family history writing?

Sometimes you just cannot write

There are times when you cannot write. Urgent matters, unexpected events and emotional upheavals will sometimes intervene. In addition, it may be that parts of the story are less compelling and less interesting to tackle at this time. Leave it and go back to it later. Write what you can now and leave what you cannot until you feel more interested, more informed and more confident.

Using quotes

Writing history necessitates that you understand and write about concepts larger than the family. To set the scene for a larger idea or event around the family, you can use quotes. Use a quote focusing on a historical era, or a historical event or an idea, to write about your family more broadly. For example, if you are writing from oral stories passed down in the family, a unifying and energising quote might be the following from Harold Pinter:

The past is what you remember, imagine you remember, convince yourself you remember, or pretend to remember.[1]

The quote tells the reader that memory is fallible but it is all we have sometimes to tell our stories in family history. The quote reminds you as the writer to be aware of this fallibility in your interpreting of the family oral stories and at the same time, value and make judicious use of all of the source material in your collection.

In *A Colonial Woman: The life and times of Mary Braidwood Mowle,* Patricia Clarke uses quotes at the beginning of chapters to introduce the dominant theme. For example, in a section titled 'Father', she uses the quote 'duty necessarily has no love', and for the chapters under the overall title 'The Desolate Years', she writes '. . . shall I ever experience the blessings of . . . riches again?'[2] These quotes are all the more poignant and relevant as they are from Mary Braidwood Mowle's diary.

Example

After my mother died in early 2005, I wrote a story 'I'll take you home Kathleen . . .' for an anthology, *Remembering Mothers*, published by the Northern Rivers Family History

Writers' Group. I wrote about Mum as a single parent and focused my story on the early years of her marriage, a marriage she found difficult and finally left.

As Mum's carer for those last years, it was often difficult to find the time or the energy to write. At the same time, being a carer enriched and changed the way that I did finally write. The following examples come from the beginning and final parts of that story:

> When my mother was dying her dementia spiralled out of control, her constant cry a heartbreaking recitation, over and over, of *take me home, please* she would say, *please can I go home.* All I could do was say *yes, I'll take you home tomorrow* or *when the sun comes up* or *on Monday* or whatever I could think of. Sometimes home was the place she lived when she had small children, and at other times, it was much further back in time when she was that untroubled teenager with her sisters and brothers on the family farm. She would sit on the side of the bed tears spilling from her eyes, repeating the words over. Mum was always heartbroken she could not go, and I was in despair that I could not comfort her. She worried that her children were at home without her, that her family did not know she was sick, or that she had to go to work. All her life Mum believed that the long past held the secret of her happiness, it was where she had been protected and young, when she had been free and full of hope. *It ended* she said *when she married.*[3]

In Mum's story I go on to relate the detail of a marriage she believed was a 'failure', her feelings of abandonment by her mother, the birth of children and tragic deaths of some children. But mostly the story is about my mother's regrets and about how she survived as a single parent in the 1950s. I also wanted to show that, despite Mum's negative reminisces which seemed to increase with her age, she did survive well and had happier times that I could write about:

Mum's journey through life, her feelings of abandonment, her difficult marriage were not, in the end, a fate worse than death even though it was a saying she used often to describe how she felt about her life and its complexity. There is little doubt her young married life was hard and difficult. She yearned to overcome that past or at least the parts of it that caused her such deep abiding regret but could not forget it. Mum's generation were hard on themselves; they saw their life events in stark uncompromising terms, as black or white, with little of the nuances we allow ourselves today. They blamed themselves for decisions that went wrong, for what they saw as tragic mistakes, which were really often just crooked stitches in the tapestry of a much lived and full life. Mum left Dad in January 1956 and she lived for almost another half century mapping out a life of hard work, personal independence and financial security. Mum was happiest when she was working, when she was busy, and when she was doing something for her family. Mum worked for the Education Department as a cleaner for more than twenty-five years. She was active in her trade union. She was involved in her community. She could embroider, knit and crochet better than anyone else I know. She sewed every item of clothing we wore as children on her treadle sewing machine. I treasure the Waltons Electric Sewing Machine she bought in the 1970s to replace it. She enjoyed good times with friends and family. She was proud of her independence and her ability to survive on her own.[4]

Writing about my mother's life was an emotional writing journey for me, sometimes painful, at other times exhilarating and always compelling. I had written parts of the story many years ago. Other parts were written after her death. In between these times I came to terms with her story, first as a daughter, then as her carer and finally as a writer. It is a journey we all take to be more informed, compassionate and more professional writers. We write different histories at each point of our journey, as we encounter not just the results of our research, but also our own emotional responses to the complicated and contradictory histories of our family's lives.

EXERCISES

- Are you a family historian? Are you a researcher? Write down a list of all of the roles you play within the family, within your social group, at work and in the community. Are you a writer, too?

- Look at the barriers to your writing as entry points for more creative and committed writing.
- Make time for your writing but remember it needs to fit within family, work and community commitments already in place.
- How you write, and what sort of family history you publish, will be determined by emotional decisions you make about how you and your family connect to that past. What emotional decisions have you made about the past? How are these reflected in your writing?

The writer is you

Negotiate, shape and orient your writing self within your family, work and community commitments.

Think of yourself as a writer. You can write part-time, or leave the writing for months on end, and still be a writer. Writing is a complex and often lonely enterprise. But it is your journey, your writing, and you can shape it to suit your story, your hopes and your dreams about family history.

Chapter three ⁀

RESEARCH AND
WRITING GO TOGETHER

K eep researching but start writing now. Read on to find out how writing as you do your research can ease the writing process.

Collect until you drop syndrome

The belief that you must collect *everything* relating to the family history is the 'collect until you drop' syndrome. This principle assumes that every piece of evidence can be found.

We might like to think we could find every document or be told every story about our family but we cannot.

At best, you will find only those records that have survived. The family letters that were not thrown away and the bits and pieces scrounged from the back of our grandparents' wardrobe, if found, will be invaluable for writing our stories.

The seductive task of collecting more certificates, more dates, ever more names, obituaries and other data associated with your family history—the piling up of the hundreds of documents until they spill willy-nilly from your home/office/garage/computer— and the satisfaction as you smugly say, 'I've got sixteen boxes of documents on top of my wardrobe and there is still more . . . !' is the 'collect until you drop' syndrome.

This syndrome affects all historians from time to time. I have worked and studied alongside doctoral students who spent so much time collecting more and more facts for their own satisfaction that by the end of their candidature they were doomed . . . to never writing it.

I have talked to historians who, although able to complete their writing task at the end, are also overwhelmed and seduced by the wonder and joy of collecting.

Who among us would not like to visit another interesting library collection and search for that elusive piece of information that we believe will complete the jigsaw puzzle of our complicated family history research?

Collecting data for historical research resembles detective work on a criminal case. Each piece of new data you find has further evidence in it about the family you are researching and from this clue or perhaps from several clues, you will make assumptions and draw conclusions leading to another line of research or another enthralling puzzle to solve.

Like a detective, you make deductions that allow you to map out where other evidence might be found, where hard-to-find information might be located. You join together pieces of incomplete data that when read as a whole will make more sense for the family history. And you begin to enjoy that detective journey very much.

There is no doubt that collecting as many of the available documents is important. We have all had that 'aha' moment when just the tiniest new piece of data made the jigsaw of complicated events finally fall into place.

However, it is also important to begin the interpretive task, examine each document in relation to other research material, and test your facts, ideas and assumptions against other historical versions of the past.

Without interpretation, your documents remain an uncoordinated, unedifying collection that is of little use in the writing process that you will follow to begin the family history.

Writing as you research will help to make both the writing and the research more focused and more professional.

Keep researching and start writing

'How can I organise and write from so much collected data?' The answer might be: Write early, write quickly and write with passion. In addition, *begin your writing at the same time as you do your research*.

Research and writing go together. You will write more easily and write better history if you begin your writing at the same time as your research. If you wait until the paper and computer piles are too great, there is no doubt they will overwhelm you.

Oh dear, I can hear you say, but I have started researching, indeed, I am almost finished. How can my writing begin easily now? Do not panic. Even if you have finished your research there will be other forays still to be made to libraries and archives as you finalise names, dates and the inevitable gaps. And you can begin to make an outline or plan from the research already done.

Keep on writing as you do your additional research and you will add much to your writing and research tasks. As you write and do the research, you will familiarise yourself with characters, with documents, with the events of your family history—and you will see the gaps sooner, and be able to determine much earlier whether to fill the gaps or leave them and move on to other research.

- Putting pen to paper makes for easier writing in your own words, linking ideas and collected facts to the family story you want to tell, at an early stage.
- Putting pen to paper early will link your reflections about the stories more strategically and effectively to your writing.
- Putting pen to paper will encourage you to look closely and critically at your ideas, research, planning, sources and constructions of the family history.

- Putting pen to paper begins the preliminary planning you should be doing for the family history at an early and therefore more effective stage.

Writing as you do your research

Begin your writing now. Take notes, and write down impressions of places you visit and of the people you talk to. Write about the research problems you encounter. Begin writing short biographies of individuals in your family history, write down stories you know about, and start making a plan. Do this while you continue your research: research and writing go together and you should be writing, in one form or another, all of the time.

Good writing is about rewriting, and everything you write as you move along the research journey will change as you gather new information and as you become more knowledgeable about your family's past.

By writing early you are writing drafts, you are completing summaries, perhaps chapter outlines, jotting down ideas—it does not have to be a final product.

This early writing is a beginning, the first draft. This writing is your beginning journey, it opens another window into easier writing, and will help to break down that awful barrier of feeling the job of writing the family history is just too much.

Instead of being only a research detective as you find a new piece of evidence, you also become a thoughtful writer, researcher and family historian. As you write these first notes and drafts or summaries, you find yourself saying, I can use that point to begin my story or perhaps it will fit with later ideas and musings.

There is nothing magical about this process. It is simply that you will benefit as a writer and researcher if you write early and write as you continue to do your research.

Making sense of your documents

As historians, we do not write from a blank page. We construct our histories from the innumerable pages of our sources, be they oral, written or electronic. Making sense of these sources so as to write more easily is the first firm step to writing family history.

Our basic tools of trade are the many documents, names and dates, land records, family stories, research notes, press cuttings, obituaries and certificates — the countless pieces of your past that you invariably collect and try to make some sense of to write the family stories.

How you make sense of the many and varied historical documents that form part of writing family history is a fundamental task encountered by students of history everywhere.

You can use genealogical software programs to sort basic names and dates. These entries then form the basis of charts, alphabetical indexes of names, reports or a family tree, and can provide the data for basic summaries of your family histories. Genealogical software cannot write the family stories for you, however, nor look at your documents and extract the information required for the stories you want to write.

Writing the text is your task, and not one you can allocate to a software program. It is your job to examine documents, reflect on family stories, make connections and assumptions about events, characters and ideas, and put them all together into a coherent whole.

Developing notekeeping skills

Underpinning your research and writing with good notekeeping skills can help minimise the task of making sense of your many documents.

Whether you copy notes by hand or photocopy your documents, the source of your information should be noted accurately and ideally include the following details:

- Author name/s, including initials
- Book or journal article
- Year, publisher and place of publication

- Page numbers (for articles, newspaper reports, bulletin excerpts, etc.)
- Name of the library or archive and any individual contact/s associated with your research of them
- File or catalogue number (if archive material)
- Folio number or record series (if archive material).

Begin your style sheet with the spelling of names, places or institutions, hyphenated words, abbreviations, and whether words are capitalised. A style sheet also ensures you record correct details for footnoting and referencing.

In addition, as you record and make detailed notes on source material, greater familiarity with your data will ease and improve how you write. Genealogical societies provide free advice on notetaking and the recording of sources on their websites. For example, see the United States Genealogical Professional Standards information on notetaking and the professional and ethical use of source material for writing family history at their website: <http://www.ngsgenealogy.org/>.

Sorting, sifting and classifying

If you decide that all you want to do is produce a detailed list of names and dates through the generations, perhaps with biographical material inserted at strategic points, a genealogical software program can help you to do this.

A genealogical software program is a sophisticated database and can facilitate the storage, recording and reporting of data. It can also format text and help you to compile and design a basic book. But, only you can compose text, write stories, and think and plan how your book will be written, formatted, shaped and published.

The mechanical task of recording and entering data into a genealogical software program can ease the burden of sorting your information, but eventually you will proceed to the next step: the analytical and interpretive task where you begin to examine your documents for themes, events, ideas, assumptions and stories from which to begin your writing.

The first step is to read and re-read your documents, and draw from your reading significant ideas, themes and stories about the family. Most family historians will use this strategy to fill out the stories of how families coped in depressions, what they did as farmers or as miners working during lean times, how they responded to war or the ravages of disease, or during floods, and other significant events.

You will want to know how women and children lived out their lives. For example, the purchase of food and food preparation without refrigeration or proper storage took up a major part of every woman's day. Childhood illness, disease and the everyday complications of child development had to be faced. There are hundreds of questions you can ask and answer through a thorough reading of your most basic documents. A list of various themes and questions for more sources and ideas can be found in Chapter 12.

The first rule here is to forget about doing it all. Faced with the prospect of sorting, organising, planning and writing everything all at once, and doing it immediately—a mammoth task—it is easier to give up.

Break down the process into manageable tasks. See your notetaking as a first step in the writing process, write as you do your research, and embark on the easy, systematic steps for making sense of your documents right now.

Filling in the gaps—later!

Filling in the gaps later is a useful rule of thumb. As you research and write, you become more knowledgeable and more familiar with your sources, and can more easily see where the gaps are.

The problem of 'filling in the gaps' in family history is especially evident when writing about women ancestors. I found this when researching both convict and immigrant women in my family. Often the only information I could find on convict women was

> linked to the birth and death of children, or her association with a male partner.
>
> Immigrant women, more likely to be unmarried and not easily found in available records, are more difficult again. I did the painstaking task of combing through possible shipping lists, checked newspapers and the records associated with their work. In addition, it was useful to look at the lives of close work colleagues, women friends, sisters, brothers, parents, neighbours and the local community.

The more research and writing you do the better able you will be to decide which gaps are important and which are not. Why spend time on unimportant detail now? Close examination of your documents and early writing will provide more clarity on where to go with further research.

As noted earlier, filling in gaps can lead to writing that is more imaginative. Certainly take note of the gaps, and in some cases you will want to fill them immediately. But take your time and enjoy the writing journey as you do your research. And begin your writing now.

Write about solving your research

Writing about the research journey you take as a family historian can add immeasurably to your final story. Readers, including your family and other historians, will want to know how you found that elusive document, or how you solved the riddle of Great Uncle George's hasty retreat to another country or state.

Tell the reader about your first visit to your grandmother's birthplace, and about the landscape, the people you meet, and the disappointment you feel when names are missing from that important shipping list.

Write about how you work through the puzzles and problems. Your readers will be interested to know what research you used to find out where the house that suddenly appears on a birth certificate was located.

Tell them about the local historical society or the museum that provided additional sources or was able to help with information. Write about your frustration as you delve further and further into a story only to find out much of it was a fabrication.

Write about your physical journey, too. And the difficulties and delights of researching in large national archives and libraries as you pick your way through intricate cataloguing and shelving systems that can sometimes seem to defy all logic at first.

Readers do not want to know everything about your research journey, but there are significant research problems that you meet and find solutions for that add to your story. They also provide important information for researchers following in your footsteps. So include them in your written family history.

There is no right way to write

Writing is a personal enterprise. It is something you do to suit your research journey as a family historian. There is no right way to write. It is only by writing and rewriting that we learn our craft. It is your writing, your plan, your family history.

In the end, how you write must be your decision. In *Alice in Wonderland*, when Alice asked which way she ought to go, the Cheshire cat replied, 'That depends a good deal on where you want to get to'. This is good advice for writers, too. Which way you go about your writing depends a good deal on where you want to get to. Remember, you are the writer, and only you know where you want to go with your writing. The next chapter will help you do this by providing specific questions to help you work out where it is you're going and the strategies you need to get there easily and professionally.

However, you will write with greater professionalism if you take note of and draw on the range of advice of other writers and family historians.

Example

The following excerpt is from a family history, 'Caroline's Story', where the author, Dorothy Simson, included much of her physical, emotional and actual research journey in the text. The end result is a delightful mix of memoir, family history and a record of the research and writing journey:

> In my garden I have a small concrete ornamental statue of a girl reading a book. She is sitting on two thick cushions which are decorated with tassels. I have her placed beside my dark green glazed garden pots. The larger pot is planted with a cream variegated willow and the smaller pot has a Dipladenia with rose coloured flowers and glossy dark green foliage. The pale grey of the girl presents an interesting contrast to the dark green of the pots, and at certain times of the day she is under the shade of the willow—a perfect place to while away a summer afternoon reading a book. She was called Caroline by the manufacturer, but I too have a Caroline, a very special person in my ancestry. She had a story to tell—which she never really told—why?[1]

The author goes on to tell an engrossing story about her great grandmother, Caroline, who was silent about her marriage to a man who was already married and who deserted her after eleven years to return to his 'first' wife. She writes how this secret became a family secret, and how her research journey, negotiated around this secret and through a process of acknowledging it, is integral to her telling of the family histories.

Simson's story of the Miskin family is compelling and well-written, and all the more readable because of the author's research journey included in it.

EXERCISES

- Establish a file where you can place written stories and notes, and add to these as you proceed with your research and writing.

- As you research and encounter problems then solve them, write these problems down and into your story, because they too now form part of the family history. Occasionally you will come up with an idea that will help to solve a research or writing problem—write it down immediately as you are likely to forget it as new information crowds into your journal and your mind.

- Keep a journal or diary to record names of libraries or individual contacts. Make notes in the diary about research to be done, people or organisations to be contacted and places to be visited.

- 'Caroline's Story' began with the tantalising sentence: 'She had a story to tell—which she never really told—why?' Write one or two paragraphs linking one aspect of your research journey to the discovery of new family history data, or alternatively your frustration at finding nothing, again. Or perhaps write about your joy as you set out to delve headlong into the records of a local library or the state records office, or open with your feelings of anticipation at another document or certificate arriving in the mail that may provide the missing link.

Start writing now

Writing is a complex undertaking and there is no doubt we would probably prefer to continue that seductive journey of researching, collecting names and dates, and busily moving from one piece of data to the next. We become experts at research long before we think about how we are going to write.

Keep on researching because this is your primary task, but begin your writing early; or if you are already well into the research, begin to think about the writing process now. Do some planning, look at your notes, sort the material, read and re-read those important documents, and begin the interpretive journey too. Begin your writing now!

Chapter four ᐳ—

WHO ARE YOU
WRITING FOR?

Who are you writing for? What will they want to see in the published family history? How does this affect the approach you choose to adopt in your writing?

Who are your readers?

The question of whom you are writing for in family history may seem straightforward. For most, the reply is: *I am writing for the family.* If you decide to publish and sell the family history, your family will be the market as well.

Certainly, your family will be uppermost in your mind as you write and think about how the final story should be produced. It is important, however, to ask additional questions as the planning and writing proceeds.

Are you writing for family?

'Are you writing for the family' should also be asked from your point of view as the author, as well as from the perspective of your potential readers.

Sometimes there may be a difference of views in the family about how the history should be written. There may be a divergence of opinion between your potential readers, i.e. your family, and you as the writer of the family history.

Your family might expect to see a more traditional format for the family history. They might prefer a detailed listing of names, dates and family events, and meticulous recording of the family genealogy from the long past to the present day.

You, on the other hand, see a different story emerge as you research and write. Your mother's or your grandmother's life story now absorbs you, or perhaps you want to write a family history about some conflict or drama that engages and grips your imagination.

Many family historians face this dilemma. A close colleague, born in England but with Irish ancestry, found that as he researched he constantly wrestled with the question of how he would finally write and publish the family history. He had completed extensive research into the English and the Irish parts of the family history, and was given considerable help by relatives who still lived in England. Having lost his mother as a very young man, however, he was interested in writing more specifically about her life as well.

When this family historian did write the story, he found

himself torn between wanting to write a story about his mother and writing a more traditional family history for his family. Do both, I said. So he did. He wrote a traditional family history for his family and is now happily working on the life story of his mother.

Writing a traditional story first can provide a substantial, detailed template for further writing. It is a record for the family. It can also be a useful source book for further research and writing.

Different writing, different readers

Do not get caught in the trap of thinking you have to do one history at the expense of another.

Ideally, you should establish a writing approach, the generations you intend to include and what time periods are appropriate, as soon as possible. Keep in mind, your family history is not everything in that past, and there will be opportunities for you to write more stories later.

Perhaps, in this instance, you are writing with the help of another family member. This approach will dictate what kind of family history you will finally publish.

I know of many family historians who have extended family contributing financially and in other ways to the family history. In such cases the final publication may need to reflect the input of many authors and contributors, and incorporate a diverse number of viewpoints. This approach can lead to a traditional format as you 'compile' the many family contributions into a coherent whole. The final publication will be finalised over time (hopefully), after many discussions with your co-authors and co-contributors.

But do not think you have to stop writing. This is just the beginning. By all means work with family members and produce a family history that most family members are happy with. But now it is your turn! There are other family stories to write. You can build on the knowledge gained from your writing to date and turn to producing a creative work of your own.

Including basic information

Whatever form your family history is finally published in, your family will want to see basic information such as names, dates, charts and maps. They will want to see their names, especially if you have consulted them about the family history and they have helped to find elusive information. They will be disappointed if you leave out this basic data.

If you are sharing the research and the writing with other family members, the final shape of the family history will depend on their needs as well as your own. Have your discussions about these points early on in the research and clarify with your fellow researchers or writers how the family history should be written.

In particular, decide how extensive the lists of names and dates will be and where you will put them in the final publication. A family chart can be a brief one page at the beginning of the work to help readers, with more detailed information placed at the end of the book. It is possible to place longer lists in an appendix. Maps and photographs are more useful if placed near to the text they relate to.

If you are the sole author and contributor to the family history writing, it will, of course, be your decision on which approach to take and in what format to publish. At the same time, extended family will have a view on how their family and their ancestry is included, and more so if they have contributed financially or by providing specific stories or research data on the understanding that it will be incorporated. Other family members who have provided valuable oral history have the right to know how their stories will be used and should be given a general outline on how these will be included in the final publication.

There are issues of privacy, ethics and how to handle sensitive material. There are also obligations you have as a historian to the discipline of history. These obligations are discussed at various stages of this book.

Practising safe genealogy

Your family will want to see the long lists of names, dates and stories they have contributed to the publishing enterprise.

It is your task, however, to ensure you have the permission to do so for all living descendants.

There was a time when we compiled extensive lists of names from the long past and linked these, through the generations, to the names, dates and lives of our grandchildren and, at times, other people's grandchildren. We blithely published these long lists in books or on the internet. Such practices are no longer acceptable in family history.

Privacy laws, and a growing awareness of the ethics involved in publication of other people's names and family data, have introduced more caution into our current practices as family historians.

The ethics of publishing other people's private information has always been an issue for professional historians. The strategy of using 'non de plumes' or an alias or a different name or simply leaving out the name has been commonly used by historians to protect living people and to protect themselves against litigation.

Since the introduction of the *Privacy Act 2000* by the Commonwealth Government and similar acts and provisions in Australian states (and overseas), the need to be sensitive to such rules and legal issues has increased tenfold.

Genealogists, like all historians, have a special responsibility to the persons they are writing about.

Although as private individuals family historians are not subject

to the *Privacy Act 2000*, there are implications if you are publishing information about living persons.

There is overlap from privacy to issues of libel, permission and other legal matters, and, of course, ethics that have always been part of all good history writing and publication.

Family history organisations and many individual family historians now consider it undesirable, indeed unethical, to publish names, dates or other information about living persons unless they have specific permission to do so. It is not sufficient to indicate that 'his mother' or 'their grandmother' or 'their children' gave permission for an individual's name to be published. Every living person in the list must give you written permission to publish their name and other data associated with them.

Defamation laws in Australia and overseas can be used if a writer lowers or damages the reputation of a living person. Because something is 'true' is no defence under Australian legislation. Overseas defamation laws vary and are complex. Obtaining permission to publish details of a living person in your family history is therefore important and ensures that what you write is not defamatory.

There are websites that cover this issue including the Commonwealth Attorney General's Fact Sheet on Privacy and Genealogy (click on Departmental Responsibilities and then Privacy): <http://www.ag.gov.au/agd/www/Agdhome.nsf>.

Legal and ethical issues are also prominent in other countries and you should be aware of these if you intend to publish information about individuals from outside Australia.

The Australian Federation of Family History Organisations (AFFO), the Society of Australian Genealogists (SAG), and other Australian and overseas family history organisations and concerned individuals have developed policies and published these on the internet.

For example, Jo Mitchell has written an overview of privacy issues for American family historians and offers the free use of her logos to place on your website as a reminder to researchers and writers in the field: <http://homepages. rootsweb.com/~cregan/privacy.htm>.

Many other Australian and overseas organisations have also developed ethical and privacy codes, and guidelines for family history societies and individuals. These are free to download at:

- AFFO's advice on privacy,
  <http://www.affho.org/info/info14.php>
- AFFO's code of ethics,
  <http://www.affho.org/affho/ethics.php>

- Guidelines For Publishing Web Pages on the Internet Recommended by the National Genealogical Society, <http://www.ngsgenealogy.org/comstandweb.cfm>
- Standards For Sharing Information With Others Recommended by the National Genealogical Society, <http://www.ngsgenealogy.org/comstandsharing.cfm>

Place of origin

It is certain that your family will want to read about the origins of the family. Historical detail about, and some analysis of why, the family left their place of origin are a staple part of beginning to write our family histories. The place of origin for Indigenous Australians will differ from those arriving on convict ships and also from recently arrived migrants from South East Asia, Southern Europe, New Zealand, the Pacific Islands or South Africa. However, the need to know about those origins will be there for all family historians irrespective of where their earliest ancestry might be found.

As the chronicler of the family origins, you can find passion, useful themes and interesting data when you seek out this ancient past. Keep the focus on your family, however, and do not be tempted to rewrite the history of 'everything' as you delve into Scottish, English, Irish, German, Italian, Chinese, Maori, Vietnamese or Indigenous Australian history for the first time.

Try to determine the historical details of village, town or farm life, and what these might have been like for the original family. You might have detailed information on these origins from letters, obituaries or other documents and be able to write with some authority. Or in some cases, oral history may provide the stories, myths, legends and family detail to begin writing.

For example, if you have Irish origins, the famine in Ireland was an important event for families. Look at the time of births, marriages and emigration, in relation to the famine, and speculate how it might have affected your family's decisions in Ireland and when they left. Not everyone who lived in Ireland, however, was similarly affected by the famine or the sectarian conflict. Just writing abstractly about those events is not sufficient.

Look at the ages of your ancestors at certain historical periods. What do you think might have been the impact of historical events, such as famine, on women and children? How did employment opportunities differ? Try to look at your family in context—the reality of their daily lives, if they were farmers, miners or merchants. What can you find out about, or examine in relation to, neighbours and surrounding community, and how these affected or were important to your family?

Stay focused on the family when you write about their origins. Someone else has already written the history of the country or the city they once lived in. You do not have to do it again. Your writing will be easier to understand and more authentic if you do not get lost in a morass of unedifying, unrelated history.

Biographical data

Your family will want to see biographical data in the finished history. They will want to read the biographies of interesting characters.

Biographical data, like your pedigree charts, are useful building blocks for later writing. They are great starting points for first-time writers and for easier writing later, and it is likely they will form an important part of the final structure of your planned book.

There is no doubt that rogues, rascals, failures, difficult people, villains and convicts make for interesting reading, but so do the ordinary characters in our family past. Women and children's lives are often neglected. Try and write them in.

If you are new to writing, you can begin your writing task by constructing biographies. File them away and insert them into the more complete family history later.

What is unique about the family?

Readers will want to know what is unique about the family. Family stories, legends and myths will help you here.

Do not confuse 'uniqueness', however, with extraordinary. Not all people are extraordinary but most are unique in some way, if ordinary.

Uniqueness can be related to culture, occupation, character, personality, different or difficult family relationships, or the 'happenstance' of family lives. There might be musical or artistic talent to write about. There may be criminal aspects too, such as forgery, bigamy and murder, although these are rarer. We would all like to find such skeletons to write about.

But in the main, the unique character of your family history will be less startling than that. It may be something to do with family conflict. Or, more specifically, how that conflict was resolved, or in many cases never resolved but left as the unhappy undercurrent of family life. Each of us will have a story to tell about how conflict, drama and unresolved family breakdown continue to affect, even if only partially, family members today.

Photographs of family

Your readers will want to see photographs. They will be delighted to see images of houses, of people, of towns, workplaces, landscape, maps, domestic life and of children at play.

Photographs are the visual windows into the past. Place them carefully so that your reader can relate them to the text.

Ask your printer, publisher or the person who is going to

reproduce your book how they want the photograph supplied for production: a digital image, a black and white (glossy or matte), or perhaps a negative. In most instances, a black and white (or colour) glossy print is the best option, and the printer or publisher will do the scanning with more superior technology than most of us have at home. Check first before you spend a lot of time producing very poor quality, and often not very useful, digital copies. More advice on photographs is found in Chapter 13.

The why of the family

Ask questions. Writing good family history is always, in the end, about asking questions. Your family will want to know the answers to questions about their ancestors. In some cases, they will supply the answers; as the family historian, it is your job to sort these out and interpret them for the final publication.

Why did your ancestors emigrate? Was it to find a better life? Was it to seek greater prosperity? Was it to escape persecution? Was it to escape the law? Was it to seek out better health, education and living conditions for their children? Was it to find gold? Was it to escape political unrest? Was it to escape poverty? Or, was that long journey away from home an amalgam of all of the above?

The 'why of the family' is an important question to ask at every point along the writing of your family history. At the beginning, your questions will be about why a young couple or a family would leave the home, the place of their birth, their parents and their friends to travel across the world to an unknown fate. Later in the story, your questions focus on other parts of the family—the events of family life in frontier towns, or their survival in small country towns.

Example

In the book *Memories & Dreams,* I focused primarily on a biography of my great grandmother using her life and work as a midwife as the focal point of my writing. I did include the family history, and placed a brief chart at the beginning of the book and a map to show the reader where various small towns were located on the Upper Macleay where the family lived.

I did not include names of living descendants except for my mother and her brother and these with their permission. The 'origins' chapter I finally titled 'Irish Dreams'. As I researched Mary Kirkpatrick's life, I felt I could write that she did have dreams and hopes as she left Ireland for New South Wales in 1884. I began the chapter with a quote from Kathleen 'Kitty' Laney, the daughter of a nurse who had worked for Mary Kirkpatrick, to set the 'scene' for the writing of this chapter:

> She spoke about her home in Ireland. I was intrigued. I said I wish I could go there and Nurse said, 'Oh no Kitty . . .

we would not sit here like this in Ireland with the doors and windows open. We had to shut ourselves in, draw the blinds, because you could be shot in your own home. So, you are lucky to live in Australia.[1]

Kitty's memories are of her childhood and visiting Mary Kirkpatrick as she aged. It is significant that she would recall such powerful words spoken by my great grandmother about the conflict in Ireland. The story of political unrest my great grandmother recalled the family would continue to remember, telling it over and over again, keeping it safely in family lore. Nonetheless, despite this deeply held social and political memory, Mary Kirkpatrick was to live most of her life in Australia, more than 60 years, and her allegiances did finally shift to this new coast, these new surrounds, new work and new friends. Her Irish origins were important to her, of course; and her childhood, her growing up and her marriage in Belfast created important aspects of the person, the character, she was to become. But it was a childhood she did not talk about, so those moments are now lost to the family, and to history.

Sadly for the chronicler of family stories, children rarely record and write their own histories. And when as adults we reflect on those childish years, we recall the tiny pieces of that past imperfectly. We filter our memories of childhood through a prism of mostly ambiguous notions about family and human relationships. We are cautious, nostalgic; we select memories that are compelling to ourselves, fitting our images of the present to those faintly held versions of the past. Mary Kirkpatrick neither talked about her childhood nor did she leave any documents or mementos that might tell a biographer something more about her life. Therefore, the childhood I have constructed for Mary is filtered through other stories, other half-remembered lives and the remnants of almost forgotten people and places. Careful research of the place of her birth added some of the colour, restored some of the long-forgotten details of her family life, and hopefully provided a picture of her childhood, and origins, in Northern Ireland.[2]

EXERCISES

- Write down some beginning stories, biographies and anecdotes. It does not matter how they are written, how polished they are or whether they make sense. File them away for revision later.
- Ask as many questions as possible as you examine your documents or listen to oral history. What period of history did your ancestors live in? What changes happened, to them and to their environment, as they grew to adulthood, married or became workers? Did they experience poverty or difficult times? Were there good times? Did they find the move to Australia offered more opportunity and greater prosperity? Were there disappointments to be faced?
- Think carefully and creatively about the lives of ancestors.

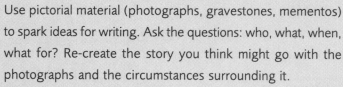

Use pictorial material (photographs, gravestones, mementos) to spark ideas for writing. Ask the questions: who, what, when, what for? Re-create the story you think might go with the photographs and the circumstances surrounding it.

• Develop hypotheses about your pictorial and other material, and test these against the historical 'facts' and more general historical context.

Find out more about readers

Talk to your intended readers. What do *they* want to see in the finished family history?

Your planning, organising and writing will be much easier if you talk to your family or readers from the outset. Do you think your story has a wider audience than the family? If so, who are they? Perhaps the local community where the family farmed, or the town where the family worked and lived, will be interested in your book.

Did you visit the local museum or historical society to do your research? Your family history could have some local history interest. It can be marketed through the local newspaper or other organisations.

Is your family history focused on an interesting occupation? Are there sailors, soldiers, midwives, public servants, politicians, teachers, lighthouse keepers or sportspersons of note in your family? A focus on one of these could take your story to a wider audience.

As we noted before, there may be many stories for you to write. Continue your writing journey now.

In general, readers of family history want to find:

- Basic information—like names, dates, genealogical charts and maps
- Place of origin
- Biographical data
- What is unique about the family
- Photographs
- The 'why' of the family.

Chapter five ᐁ

ASKING QUESTIONS AND FINDING IDEAS

Asking questions is a key strategy for writing professional family history. The more questions you ask the easier it will be to write and write well.

Why ask questions?

Writing good family history is about asking questions. Often questions can be as important as answers in history. Asking questions is an excellent way of developing an outline or a plan to begin the writing of your family history.

The unique character of your family history will emerge more easily and with greater flair if you ask questions around as many topics, ideas, themes and family activities as you can. Read widely and look at other aspects of family, local, national and international history to find the questions relevant for your family history.

Family mementos

Ask questions about family mementos such as photographs, newspaper clippings, furniture, kitchen objects (e.g. teacups, teapots, cutlery), jewellery, and crochet and knitting patterns. Examine cookbooks, recipes, books, letters, diaries, invitations, cards, bibles and prayer books. Assess drawings, sewing books, medical or health guides, stamp collections, trophies and prizes, and certificates of merit.

Photographs are the most prized find of the family historian, particularly if they are prints of generations before great grandparents. Photographs can also provide clues to family relationships, landscape, clothing, jewellery and the dynamics of family life.

You can be surprised by small discoveries in images: the way a woman wears her hair, the tilt of the head, the hand resting on a shoulder, the youthfulness of faces, the strength and toughness in a gaze, the formal clothes, or the bare, dirt floors. Books, newspaper cuttings, kitchen objects, recipes, domestic embroidery and sewing give many clues to family interests, schooling, parenting, family relationships and everyday living.

Family stories

Ask questions about courtship, romance, family meetings and family conflict. How did the family fare during the Great Depression, world wars or economic downturns, and were there unusual events or adventures to recall? Ask about music, song, dance, recitation, legends, myths, nicknames, colourful sayings, beliefs and superstitions.

Family stories are the most logical and useful beginning for writing family history. Write them down. Do not be deterred by comments about the unreliability of memory—a simple way to check their veracity is via birth, death and marriage certificates and other official records. Family stories provide the colour and add the vibrancy to set your family history apart from others.

These stories may not be factually correct, and each of us must be aware that time may give some distortion or that family members may attempt to whitewash or embellish the stories. The stories will provide leads to further research, however, and this may establish authenticity in time. If authenticity is difficult to establish, record the stories anyway with the proviso that the facts are unsubstantiated to date.

Family traditions

To enliven your text and add the unique flavour of your family history, try to find out the family stories and family traditions that have become integral to it. Did your original ancestors bring traditions from their overseas origins and retain them, at least in part?

Other family traditions centre on cultural activities—the English concern with morality and manners, the Scottish focus on clans. What cultural traditions did your ancestors bring to Australia and how did they retain or modify them?

Visit the National Library's Folklore and Oral History Unit website <http://www.nla.gov.au/oh/howtoohist.html>. It holds a range of material focusing on Australian music, culture, song, dance, folklore and oral history traditions collected and recorded since the 1950s. Look also at books and resources in local and state libraries focusing on folklore and family traditions.

Family relationships

Look for cards, diaries, mementos of love and romance, gifts, letters, holiday souvenirs, postcards, photographs, and family stories. Close examination of marriage and re-marriage can provide a rich source of information about family relationships.

Researching people who live nearby or are near relatives in a person's life can provide starting points for writing. Women's lives, in particular, are more difficult to find sufficient detail about, and researching the men and women around them can provide leads, alternative sources and hopefully more information.

Look at work colleagues, friends, sisters, brothers and neighbours of your ancestor—if you do not know anything about how your ancestor lived then widen your perspective.

Examine the lives of neighbours, and the community in which your family lived. Australian towns and villages were small before 1900 and local newspapers were more likely to report on minor characters' lives. I found information in the local newspaper detailing when my great grandmother left town to visit family or when she arrived back. There were reports on fetes, fundraising and events she organised for the community.

Neither your family, nor the individuals in it, existed in isolation from their communities. There was a much heavier reliance on neighbours, close friends or family in the past; for support during difficult times or to share celebrations. Your family history publication will benefit when you also see the links and connections between families and individuals, neighbours and local community.

Family class, background and work

Family historians will find that the family, and the place of individual women, men and children in it, will differ according to culture, class, religion and race. The idealised Victorian English middle-class family favoured a restricted, private and domestic role for women, with men appropriating as their own the public spheres of paid work, governance and legal activity. In nineteenth century Australia, English middle-class manners were copied but the colonial climate could not hope to match that previous genteel lifestyle now left behind. The harsh pioneering environment introduced new challenges not just to men but to women and children as well.

The real life experiences of European and Indigenous men and women in early Australia were important to the development of colonial family relationships and the socio-economic developments which accompanied them. Women provided then, as they still do today, the emotional and physical support for the continuance of most family life.

For information on family class and social change in Australian history, see Burgman and Lee's *A Most Valuable Acquisition* and their *Staining the Wattle*; and Osborne and Mandle's *New History: Studying Australia Today*. There are useful references and sources for family historians on this and other Australian history topics at the Society of Australian Genealogists' Basics on Australian history sources website at <http://www.sag.org.au/ozsources/history.htm>.

Asking about characters

Ask questions about the names, births, origins, personal memories, work, schooling and appearance of your grand-parents and great grandparents.

Are there stories told about where they lived, how they coped during a long sea voyage (if immigrants), and how they met the changes and challenges of a new land? See Chapter 7 for more ideas and questions for writing about characters in family history.

Games, leisure, travel and holidays

Look for items that recall favourite family leisure activities such as stories about playing cards, sporting activities and achievements, mementos of family holidays, theatre and cinema tickets, and train or bus tickets.

Write about children's games and childhood experience. Include the songs, dance and music remembered from home, school and work.

You will find information and background in books such as Mark St Leon's *Spangles & Sawdust: The Circus in Australia*, and *The History of Leisure in Australia: A Bibliography*, compiled by Carmel Foley and Rob Lynch. Also see the online publication <http://www.business.uts.edu.au/lst/downloads/ 03_History_bib.pdf> and library searches on sport, and eighteenth and nineteenth century Australian travel and family holidays.

Living patterns and home life

Living patterns can be drawn from the physical arrangement of households and from the structure of houses and the way in which the family functioned in them. Some family historians have been able to find out details of household arrangements from the wills that were made, especially those from early historical periods.

For example, a father might be very specific in a will that a bed or dresser situated in a particular room in the house is *not* to be left to a particular daughter or son because that child has married into a family of whom the father does not approve. In addition, the person making the will sometimes made a very detailed list of possessions, and where they were located, so that you can, with a little imagination, reconstruct how such items fitted into the household and how they might have been used.

In the distant past, the idea of privacy with a room allocated to each child and to parents was not the norm; in fact, in the Middle Ages and in working-class homes until late in the nineteenth century, it was common for all members of the family to eat, sleep, receive visitors and take care of livestock in the one large family room. The family of nineteenth century Australia lived in a house with a minimum number of rooms and the furniture, cooking facilities and washing arrangements would have been very different to modern Australian homes.

Unfortunately, very few restored houses demonstrate how ordinary people might have lived in the past. The focus of heritage societies and museums has been to concentrate on larger buildings and the reconstruction of the large, imposing houses of the rich, the famous and the politically powerful that survive more readily than the small working-class cottage or temporary shack in the outback.

It is possible to find out a little more about how your ancestors lived by examining the functions of the houses they lived in. Look closely at the living arrangements they developed to cope with the climate, geography, isolation, lack of sanitation and other difficulties, which were simply a part of everyday life in colonial Australia.

An effective way to reconstruct an ancestor's living patterns is to look at old photographs, building plans and engravings of the time. Catalogues and trade manuals from the period under study constitute a further source.[1] From these you can familiarise yourself with the variety of household furniture items and equipment more commonly used in that period, and begin to construct in your mind a picture of the living conditions of ordinary families in early Australia. Ask questions about furniture, rooms and their furnishings, cushions, quilts, pillow shams, bed clothes, tablecloths, tea towels, samplers, wall hangings, lamps, candles, gas lighting, windows, curtains, doors and vestibules.

Information about how our ancestors lived at particular times in the past can be found through looking at other local and family histories. For some, a house may have been a simple log hut or a tent. For example, Elizabeth Sweet, accompanied by her children, arrived to join her husband at the Roper River in 1872 and lived for ten weeks in a tent while incessant rain made for a very uncomfortable stay.[2] Tent living also characterised the lives of seasonal workers. Isobel Slockee lived in a tent with her canecutter husband in the 1920s. Aboriginal and Islander women who worked at 'cutting paspalum, cutting corn or chopping bananas' were housed in humpies and subject to appalling conditions.[3]

For others a modest farmhouse with a garden or a small cottage in town could have been the norm. Davison and McConville note that homesteads rarely consisted of a single building.[4] A homestead was usually accompanied by a number of separate wooden buildings which might have housed grain, a dairy, quarters for male workers, stables, coach houses, woolsheds, the blacksmith, a killing house, a skin-drying house, bath-houses, lavatories, cow bales, dog kennels and shearers' quarters. Often, too, the kitchen was a separate building.

Religion

Religion was not a remote concept for most of your ancestors. It was a tangible part of everyday experience. For some families, religion played a daily role, with regular prayer and a strong belief in particular dogmas and religious principles. Others perhaps shunned religion or were alienated from it as transportation or immigration took them far away from the religious traditions of their past.

Your own beliefs and understandings about religion can

be traced to these early developments. Although it is sometimes difficult to reconstruct actual religious affiliations and the depth of feelings about church and faith, it might be possible through talking to older members of the family, and studying the histories of the place of origin, to relate part of the religious context of your family's history.

Did any members of your family work in a voluntary capacity for the church or for charity? Did female members participate in the Woman's Christian Temperance Union? Were there ministers of religion in your family? If so, there are numerous records in the state libraries or with the various church archives. I found many references in local newspapers to women working for the Red Cross, for church organisations, for the war effort and for other charitable causes. In small communities these events are reported in detail with names of women highlighted and are a rich source of data for writing.

Economic and political life

Not all families had the same access to wealth and power or to better paid job opportunities. Working-class and poorer families in mining communities, rural districts and the slums of Sydney were the real 'battlers' of early Australia. Ruth Park's writing in *The Harp in the South* captures their world very well.

Try to consider in your writing how your ancestors might have fared during the depression years of the 1890s and 1930s, during the world wars, and in moving from country to country or state to state. How they coped with changing economic times as industrialisation and urbanisation overtook them, changed the workplace and living conditions, and impinged on traditional family life will provide significant data for writing your stories.

Women ancestors

Many changes that have had an impact on the character of the family were associated with the changing role of women in society, especially in relation to paid work, and changing relationships between women and men within the family, in marriage and in the professions. You will write more accurately and write more interesting lives for women ancestors if you recognise their achievements and their contribution to Australian history in its fullest sense.

Domestic violence, poverty, disease and epidemics, problems in childbirth, incessant childbearing, large numbers of children to care for, household drudgery, isolation, and few economic and political rights were all characteristic of Australian women's lives. There were also positive aspects: pioneering in a new land, a better climate for the rearing of children, some freedom from the strict manners and customs of English tradition, the freedom to experiment with new foods and new ways of doing housework, a greater access to comfortable and affordable housing, and more relaxed family and religious traditions.

Women farmed beside men; women kept the accounts and partnered husbands in business ventures; male teachers' wives taught infants and girls for no salary; and the wives of male postmasters dutifully assisted behind the old wooden desk of the early post office. Working-class women worked after marriage out of economic necessity, but the preferred role for a married woman was the middle-class idealised one where women's lives were private, domestic, dependant and obedient to their husbands' needs and demands.

Many biographies of Australian women have been produced in recent years, as well as histories of the different work, home and social experience of women in Australia. There are other sources to add to your research of women: these include letters, diaries, family books, cookbooks, photographs, sewing books, other memorabilia, trophies or prizes, obituaries, divorce records, electoral rolls, directories, government publications, pioneer registers, council records, court and gaol returns, inquests, charitable records, hospital records, church records, school records and the records of women's organisations.

Women's invisibility in family history is part of a wider historical perspective, which relegates women's lives, too often, to the invisibility of neglect and omission. As family historians we are in a unique position to research, record and write about our women ancestors who were brave enough to live the most extraordinary lives. The least we can do is include their stories more vividly, in more detail and more precisely in our family histories.

Childhood years

Researching and writing about children is a difficult task because children usually have left little in the way of written records. Family historians have to rely on the evidence of adults and their perceptions of what childhood was like in the past.

Nonetheless, it is possible to include in your family history something about the children and their childhood experiences to take your depiction of family life beyond a mere list of children's names.

One way into the world of the child is to look at the games and play activities they were involved in for the historical periods under study. June Factor's book *Captain Cook Chased a Chook* is a good starting point as it describes some of the games, rhymes and play activities of children in nineteenth century Australia. Sue Fabian and Morag Loh's *Children in Australia* is a useful sourcebook on the history of childhood, including information on Indigenous children and children from working-class as well as non-English-speaking backgrounds.

Another way into the lives of children is to peruse women's history—as women had the care of children, you will find both specific and general contextual material in past and recent histories of women's lives. Autobiography and biography are useful, too, as they often focus on family and family relationships including the lives of children.

Look for school report cards, childhood friendships, achievements and awards, school uniforms, school books, school magazines, schools attended, teachers remembered, book clubs, hobbies, childhood games, sports and pets.

The most significant event in the lives of many Australian children in the nineteenth century was the introduction of compulsory schooling in the late 1870s and 1880s in every state. Before compulsory schooling, working-class children worked from an early age on their parents' farm, in factories, in mines and in domestic service. Of course, compulsion was not enforced thoroughly until the early 20th century, so for many poorer children schooling remained a brief part of their life experience anyway.

Although the children of Australia were spared the worst excesses of exploitation and the horrors of the industrial revolution in England, many did have a hard life. Young women were kept at home to help with the care of younger siblings and to support overworked mothers. Family historians should note, too, that Indigenous children in early Australia were excluded from the public school system, giving them a far different childhood experience from European children. Childhood, therefore, was not a uniform experience but differed across class, gender and race.

It is possible to find out about certain categories of children and deduce from this some of the characteristics of childhood life within your own family in the past. There were many official inquiries on aspects of childhood life, including select committees and royal commissions into destitute children, on the employment of children, on neglected children, on the various charitable institutions which took care of deserted and delinquent children, and on various aspects of formal education and training of children. All of these are found in the 'Votes and Proceedings' of the various state parliaments. Family historians will find a wealth of detail about the everyday world of the child in Australia in them.

The changing family

The notion of family has undergone change over the centuries in its membership and the relationships of individuals in it, and has adapted in response to changing governments, education, work and politics.

The traditional nuclear family of male breadwinner with a wife and children at home is no longer the dominant family group. Trial marriage, single-parent (usually female) households, merged families (of divorced women and men), and more democratic relationships between parent and child are now increasingly evident in our society. Women are marrying at a later age and are much more likely to remain childless than their mothers and grandmothers. This is particularly the case for women born since the late 1960s.

The social changes in the family and childhood point to a very different genealogy in the future. Divorce, trial marriage, co-habitation, ex-nuptial births by choice, women choosing to keep their birth names whether married or not, IVF techniques, frozen embryos (whose? who decides?), and many other factors are rapidly changing the whole face of conception, birth, proof of maternity or paternity, and marriage. None of these changes occurred overnight, however, and your recording of your family history can help to map these changes and provide new documents and new social histories about the family.

The history of the family is a kaleidoscope of cultural, familial, economic, political and ideological change that can be mapped successfully only if we recognise the multiplicity of historical events and experiences which have shaped them. Your family history is one small part of that historical change, and the way you document and tell your family story adds to our knowledge and understanding of it and the many changes that are part of it.

Example

Rose Carolyn Atkins, an Australian citizen, married the Japanese art student Moshi Inagaki in 1907. Ailsa G. Thomson Zain'uddin describes Rose's long struggle with the Australian authorities as she and her husband were made disenfranchised and stateless during World War II.[5]

The following excerpt from Rose's letter to the Alien Registration Department, written in 1940, illustrates her anger and frustration at the treatment meted out to her and her husband:

> I am an Australian woman of British parentage . . . married to my husband for more than thirty-two years. We have both been loyal citizens of the Empire and my husband has most faithfully served this State for all those years as a teacher, twenty years at the University . . . I have naturally been, perhaps violently, British. I object strongly to my treatment at the hands of a Policeman. I spoke my objection, but my fingerprints were somewhat forcibly taken. I was also told that they would be used against me. I wish to know how and why this is to be done? Is it a criminal offence to marry a foreigner?[6]

Zain'uddin's story about Rose Inagaki poses critical questions about the validity and significance of the rules of internment and denial of citizenship to individuals on the basis of racial intermarriage.[7] Rose's story, as a result, has a relevance and resonance to broader questions of immigration and citizenship which can be applied even today.

Asking such questions of your family history will add much to the bigger picture of our past.

EXERCISES

There is one story that you should write down immediately. This is the story of your life! How many times have you lamented the lack of information you have about your parents or grandparents? Do you often wish that you had talked more to elderly relatives, many of whom have now passed away and are no longer able to tell their stories? Do you also think about how much easier your job as a family historian would be if your ancestors had written down some of their life experiences to be passed on to the next generation? I know I do!

You cannot retrieve the history your ancestors did not think to record for you, but you can do something about your own history. You can record your life experiences for your children and grandchildren, and for the family and local historians of the future. It is often hard to think of our own lives as important historical documents. We tend to think about the present as uninteresting or prosaic. But, to our children and grandchildren and the historians of the future, your life story will provide some of the rich detail of Australian community life that is almost impossible to find in existing official records. Where do you begin?

Begin with as many memories you can recall about your parents and grandparents. Write down the stories your parents told you. For your life story, write down the details of your birth and try to detail the experiences of your childhood. Write about your sisters and brothers and the games of your childhood. Tell about your schooling and about the community in which you lived. Who were your neighbours? How did you travel? Did you live in the city or the bush? How did your family survive during depression times, recessions or war years?

Write about the experience of growing up and becoming an adult? Write about your work and leisure activities? Did you have special training in music or did you play sport? Write about your life experiences in the context of social and economic issues as well. Was your life different because you were female? Were you the first-born or the youngest, and how did this impact on your family relationships, your self-confidence and your personality? Did you have to go to work because of poverty in the family? Were you one of the lucky individuals who went on to higher education and was thus able to secure a place in the professions?

Write about your personal relationships and whether you married. If you have children, write about becoming a parent and how this affected your life. If you are retired write about what it is like in Australia to become an older citizen. Were you born overseas? Did you grow up in a family where English was not the main language, and where different European or Asian cultural ideas and behaviour was retained?

Writing your life story will preserve history for the future. In some respects this is somewhat like keeping a diary and you might like to start doing this as a beginning activity. It is sometimes surprising when you sit down and begin recording your life story to discover just how different or interesting your life experiences might be. Tell your children that you are writing your life story

and ask them to take care of it in the future. Encourage them to add to the family history with their own life experiences. No matter how dull or uninteresting you might think your present life story is, it is important to preserve it. Researchers and writers of family and local history in the future will be very glad that you did.

Ask questions

Write early, write quickly and begin the systematic task of asking questions that are relevant to and useful for shaping the stories in your family history. Ask questions:

- About family class and background
- About family relationships
- About games and leisure activities
- About religion
- About everyday life and living patterns
- About economics and political life
- About the lives of women ancestors
- About the changing family
- About childhood
- About landscape and geography
- About houses, buildings, towns, rivers
- About transport, communication, roads,
- About other families, neighbours, friends, colleagues.

Chapter six ᐲ

FROM BELFAST TO BELLBROOK: ORIGINS, ARRIVALS AND WRITING ABOUT THEM

Y our first arrival is your feisty pioneer. Use these origins to write passionately but critically about that long past.

Your ancestors came from where?

One of our basic research tasks as family historians is to find family origins. We may know the origins of recently arrived ancestors but are less sure of those who arrived before 1850. However, once we begin the search, compiling this information becomes an all-consuming mission. It is a compelling search we embark on. We may not know where we will be at the end of the journey but we are fascinated, indeed we are spellbound, by the story unfolding before us.

We travel back, either by the internet or in reality, to Italy, England, Ireland, Scotland, Germany, China, Africa, Vietnam or the Middle East . . . and we feel an emotional, indeed some might say a spiritual connection, to these places. Recently arrived immigrants will know their origins. This is not the case for family historians where ancestry is traced back through four or five generations in Australia. The delight when they do find their origins is layered by other emotions as they make new discoveries about who they are and how they might now relate to and understand their past.

There are many other original ancestors to be found of course. If you were to pursue every line of research on the family tree, the collected multitude of places, people and dates would be overwhelming.

But it is *this* original family that you find intriguing. Perhaps it is your mother's family that draws you in, or it is a line of descent that links into significant family traditions. Maybe these favourite original ancestors were farmers and the family are farming still, or they were merchants who seem to have instilled ideas of business enterprise into following generations. Or, you see the women in that line as connected to your life. There is no doubt you relate to the family rivalries or to the everyday family events as you encounter them in your research.

Having read the background histories of county Down, Belfast or Cornwall, or of Glasgow or Devon or eighteenth century

London, or indeed travelled to them, you could find yourself standing in the very place, perhaps in the same building, where your ancestors might have once walked, worked and lived. Similar feelings of having once known a place are reported by immigrants who left Vietnam or India or Lebanon or Greece or South America when very young or whose parents or grandparents arrived in Australia in the 1950s or 1960s.

You see the churches, the cobbled streets, thatched roofs and other historical architecture and find yourself drawn to it. You scan faded photographs and imagine how ancestors might have survived once they stepped away from the photographer's lens. Surely, you can make that next emotional leap and say that not only were they here once, but you are part of this place too. You are connected to it.

It is, of course, useful to travel and see the landscape, the buildings and the history of your past; it is an emotional and moving experience to walk in the same spaces and places where your ancestors once lived.

It can add much to your writing to imagine how men and women lived and worked. It is useful to think about how they walked the streets, cooked food, talked to neighbours and took part in church services. These people also looked after children, met new friends, engaged with the community, went to school, told stories, were happy, sad, joyful and in love, and they are your family too. You feel you know them somehow.

89

Yet, hundreds of years separate us from that time. You cannot, indeed do not, know them at all. So, what is this 'falling in love' we do with our ancestral past. Can you use these emotional triggers to ease the writing process? Yes, you can. As always, however, this emotional response to the long past should be tempered by a judicious writer's eye firmly fixed on historical sensibility, accuracy and credibility.

Fading landscapes, favourite characters

When I walked the streets of Belfast trying to locate precisely the places where my great grandmother Mary Kirkpatrick was born, went to school, married and then finally left for New South Wales, I found little left of the actual places and spaces of her childhood and growing up. Where her mother and father had met as young lovers, were married and then lived out most of their lives in Ballymacarrett was already bull-dozed and gone. The house Mary lived in after she married had been replaced by a fire station.

Public buildings like churches, schools and government offices do survive, but unless you link back to a wealthy family it is not likely you will find the house where your original ancestors lived.

Landscape changes. Even the landscape of my own childhood, spent on a small dairy farm on the mid north coast of New South Wales in the 1940s, has changed. Modest wooden houses have been demolished. Remnants of barns, dairy bales and pig runs dot a landscape that is now used to run large herds of beef cattle.

What remains, of course, in most landscapes are the rivers, hills, creeks, cliffs and rocky outcrops near the sea, or the green and blue haze of distant towering ranges; and a memory of how these shaped and were part of our family's past.

It is possible to stand beside a river in Ireland or Italy and imagine how original ancestors might have used the river, ran boats on it or perhaps built houses or workplaces near to it. But how best can you link this imaginative and emotional aspect to your research and writing journey? One way is to recognise this emotional pull to the long past, use it but cautiously so that we do not obliterate the connections it has to the present.

Falling in love with castles and cobblestones

Did I fall in love with the castles and cobblestones of Ireland? Yes, I did. The romance of Irish history and its visual representation, through cute window boxes with flowers spilling from them, the colourful boats moored strategically along canals and rivers, atmospheric pubs and innumerable castles, was irresistible.

But only with some parts of Ireland. Some of it was less inviting. Like all things, landscape is more complex than that first glimpse of romance and constructed heritage we see in the facades of villages, streets and cities in Europe.

My great grandmother lived in the Protestant parts of Belfast. I found the suburban landscape where she once lived bleak and uninviting. As I wandered the streets searching for any signs of my ancestry, the people of Belfast were struggling with the demons of the present. The peace process between Catholics and Protestants had stalled, the streets were bare and menacing, and the billboards with hooded men holding guns and threatening violence were overpowering in the city landscape.

Mary Kirkpatrick never went back to Ireland although she spoke about it often. She also talked about the violence, which was widespread when she was a child. Twenty when she left Belfast, Mary lived the next 60 years in Australia. She settled in a coastal New South Wales town that she came to love.

Still you (and I) hark back to origins as though they explain everything about our family past. We forget about the less attractive features of that past. In addition, we minimise the importance of the immigrant country in shaping our ancestor's lives. It is this focus on a simplified and romantic version of our origins that limits the value of much published family history.

Recognising limits

Where family historians also find deep emotional links for their history is in Australia. I certainly found it here in the Australian landscape where my grandparents, my mother and

I had lived in the same small coastal valley for a major part of the nineteenth century and since.

I did not find that same feeling in Ireland although, like other family historians, I would have loved it if I had been able to claim it as my own. My father's ancestors hail from Athlone on the banks of the beautiful River Shannon. This, too, I would love to claim.

Travelling back to the places and spaces where your ancestors lived can provide authenticity to your writing. Having seen the hills, the rivers, the buildings and the different climate can add confidence, credibility and vividness to your stories.

At the same time, keep your perceptions of those origins within the bounds of reality, write about the complexity of how you experience meeting your ancestors and their origins, and try to overcome unnecessary sentimentality in your writing about that long ago past.

It is a nice idea to think it is our ancestors who make Naples, or county Clare or London or Glasgow or Cairo or Palestine or the north coast of New South Wales, so central in history. In the excitement of finding a significant original ancestor in a quaint village somewhere, we forget that hundreds, indeed thousands, of other families also once lived there. Will other family historians be able to claim the same unique, significant origins as we do? Yes, they will.

Certainly, map out those origins and work out how they affect your family. Your readers will want to know about the streets, the farming community or the buildings that once might have housed your ancestors. They will be less impressed by attempts to turn your ancestors into a one-dimensional triumphant family dominating that past.

You should look at your ancestors as multi-dimensional characters who, once they left that place of origin, faced and were shaped and changed by very different emotional, psychological, familial, economic and social pressures. It is a far different world they would have experienced if they had stayed in their original country.

They were immigrants at first but soon became established settlers and families in Australia. They made their individual accommodations with a more rugged landscape, long distances, different climate and isolation. How they thought about who they were, as Irish or German, or now Australian, is more complex than just describing cute thatched houses or Gothic buildings of the past.

The 'what I am going to do in this chapter' summary

When writing about origins, a long summary at the beginning of your chapter is unnecessary and boring for the reader. The chapter needs no introduction other than the words, sentences, ideas and facts that tell its story.

If there is additional information in the summary, this too is confusing. If the information is important then place it in the text at relevant points. If it is not then leave it out.

An introductory paragraph or chapter is not a repetitive summary of the text that follows it. The first sentences and paragraphs in your chapters should aim to capture the reader's attention and ease the reader into the chapters' events.

Why not write the origins chapter about a spectacular, sad, unusual, suspenseful, unexpected, painful or enthralling anecdote or story to set the scene? Do you identify with some of the landscape? Do you feel a sense of kinship although you did not know these people? Then say so. Write about your feelings, including the doubts, the wonder and the complexity of this relationship with the long past.

The beginning paragraph, chapter or section is the connecting glue that brings the reader and the writer together. Some writers use the device of challenging or shocking the reader by juxtaposing youth with age or death against life. The following first paragraph from *The Mayne Inheritance* is a good example of such an approach:

From his early years Patrick Mayne knew what he wanted— to break out of his past into a better future. It was so when he fled the unrelieved deprivation of his youth in Ireland, and equally so as he lay dying at his Brisbane home and contemplated the terrors of the hereafter. Between his youth and his premature death is a life that was brutal, spectacular and tragic. No one can say what awfulness in the child's life directed the actions of the man.[1]

Family stories and sayings are useful starting points as in the following example from 'Not All Plain Sailing':

> 'Don't ever let the moon shine on his head or it will turn into a bucket.'
>
> This superstitious advice was given to twelve-year-old Winifred before she set out in 1919 with her father and two-year-old brother, Albert, from England, bound for Australia.
>
> Young Winifred mulled these words over as she stood on the dock waiting to board the huge ship towering before her. She felt a great responsibility towards Albert and, in her innocence, later spent many an anxious hour moving Albert's small crib around the already cramped cabin, fearful of what might befall her young charge.[2]

The poignancy of these introductory words is enhanced as we read on to learn that Winifred is sailing without a mother who had died some months earlier. Her role as a carer for her small brother, as well as providing support and companionship to her father, make her later life events a more interesting and compelling read.

Another device for an introductory piece is to begin at the end and then flash back to where the story should begin. For example, read this introduction from: 'What is a "Mother"?'

What does the word 'mother' mean to me?

As I sit quietly in meditation I reflected on my mother who was twenty-two years old when I was born. I saw a woman who was always close by, worked hard, provided a caring environment, and who fed, clothed and bathed me. A woman who comforted me when I was sick and in need of a cuddle, who taught me the necessities of life yet let me gain experience and develop and grow through the different early life stages to adulthood. I reflected too on when I became a mother and the birth of my first child.[3]

After reflecting on these issues in her first paragraphs, the author then goes on to tell the story of Joan as a child, a young woman and then as a mother and grandmother. Using an opening device such as a startling statement or an anecdote or a flashback story is a way of capturing the reader's attention and a strategy to help the writer begin their story. The unexpected, the accidental, the inspirational or the humorous can be used in this way.

The triumphant tree

The 'we won the war' or 'we had the best time' or 'we were a happy, hardworking family' or 'we had brave, strong and true ancestors' as descriptors of the family has a long tradition in Australian history.

In family history, this emerges as triumphalism in some cases, while in others it is just poorly expressed and badly nuanced history. We write that our ancestors (the Protestants or the Catholics or the Lutherans or the Chieftains or the Confederates) were the bravest, the strongest, the happiest, the hardest working or the most significant in the community.

Irish ancestry is often triumphant. With Protestant roots we write fondly of the Orange orders and their traditions, but rarely write about the other side of the conflict. If we have Catholic origins, we write of oppression and discrimination and leave our analysis at that.

When writing about my great grandmother, Mary Kirkpatrick, who was a Protestant from Belfast, I also had to consider the other side of the conflict. My father's family are from Catholic Roscommon, their history complicated by a marriage between a Protestant and a Catholic. In the introduction to my book, I wrote:

Mary was ten years old in 1872 when the first nationalist parade, led by Joseph Biggar, was held in Belfast. The same night, Protestants from Sandy Row clashed bitterly with Catholics from streets near Great Victoria Street Railway Station, the General Hospital full of the injured and maimed. That bitter conflict raged for days with increasingly violent attacks on nearby churches and houses.[4] But of course, it is difficult to find a time in Ireland, in Belfast, when there were no political troubles or religious conflicts. It is difficult to find a time when the Irish did not leave Ireland, as Mary did, to put those conflicts behind them. To leave behind the awful tensions, the bitter divisions as Catholic and Protestant alike turned on one another in the same streets in which their children walked to school, and in the same houses and churches in which they were baptised, where they were married, and where now they too often mourned.[5]

Stay away from a triumphant view of your original ancestry. Think about your family and the characters as multi-faceted. Try to determine how that period of history, the specific political and economic events, and the social contexts of the time, impacted on and shaped your family. Examine how the family felt as they left their original homeland, confronted the challenge of immigration and were changed by the diversity, difference and hope of a new land.

Example

The following excerpt is from the family story 'George Brown and Bethia Noble' by Ellen McDonald. It illustrates very succinctly how one family historian wrote about the complexity and the surprising character of some family origins.

George Brown, born in Belgium, father John, a shipwright. Ha, this should be easy. Brown in Belgium. Should stand out like a sore thumb.

On his marriage certificate and his daughter's birth certificate our George gave his birthplace as Allicallan, Belgium. After considerable research I can now say there is no such place. It appears I'm trying to track down a liar. Cousin Marie said she thought he was Armenian, which confused me even more. Then I had some luck. On a visit to Melbourne with my mother-in-law I visited a cousin from that side of the family who gave me our George's baptismal certificate, along with his photo. It transpires that George was born in Pernau, Estonia and his name was really Jurri Braumann. The plot thickens.

At this stage, the iron curtain was well and truly in place and Estonia was under Russian control. I wrote a letter in Russian to the equivalent of the county council in Pernau, which, 12 months later, brought the following reply, 'Thank you for your inquiry. We'll look into it and let you know.' They never did.[6]

Ellen MacDonald's story, apart from being a very good example of how to write about the research journey as well as the family story, demonstrates how complicated the researching of just one line of inquiry can be. It alerts us to the complexity and the uncertainty of our past and how, when we find our origins, the certainties of our perceptions about the past may quickly disappear.

Humour, suspense, surprise, loss, conflict, secrets—all of these can be writing starters for your origins chapter. They

will be there waiting among the many twists and turns on
the branches of your family tree.

EXERCISES

- Think about the connections your ancestor had to their
  homeland, to the new places they immigrated to and how this
  brings meaning to your writing? How do you feel about the
  long past, the Australian years and/or your emotional
  connections to your grandparents or great grandparents?
- What made your family distinctive in their place of origin?
  Are there unusual events or legends associated with your
  family? Write these down. Celebrate the uniqueness of
  your family's past but also see the common connections to
  other families and communities.
- Write a short story about travel in your family. Write about
  'memorable moments' in the family history.
- Draft a table of contents for your original ancestors. Link the
  relevant categories—themes, topics, events, characters—to
  other text in order to form intended or possible chapters.
- Why did you choose this particular ancestor or these origins
  to write about? Are you focusing on these origins for 'political'
  reasons? Were your ancestors more conservative or more
  radical, the most sporting group or the most successful in
  business? Tell your readers why you think you chose to write
  about them. Your story will be more honest and all the more
  engaging as a result.

Writing about the many pathways to your origins

Family stories, family mementos, and birth, death and marriage certificates are the basic tools of our research. And they offer numerous pathways to our ancestral origins.

We often focus on a line of research that appeals to us and are fascinated by stories handed down to us from parents and grandparents. The old story about descending from royalty is not accurate but there is often enough romance and mystery in it to send us on a search.

Landscape, architecture, and the legend of what once was are great story starters. So embrace the excitement of finding the places where your ancestors lived.

At the same time recognise the limits of this emotional history and imbue your family story with a critical eye for detail. Be aware that there are many pathways and a multitude of origins.

Chapter seven

A WRITING ROADMAP

Too much information, too many possible pathways? Take a break and read how a writing roadmap can help you focus and get you writing—easily!

Your writing is going where?

There will surely be books somewhere that can tell you all you need to know about writing, editing and publishing. There is ample information, too, contained on the thousands of websites on writing, publishing, editing, grammar, writing life stories, memoir and family history research.

However, even with such abundant expert advice at your fingertips, do you know where you are going with your writing? Do you know what kind of family history you want to write?

Your readers (mostly family) will influence how you finally

write, but your preferences, your ideas and your own perspective on how to put the family stories into print will be important too.

Successful writers who talk publicly about the creative act of writing sometimes forget to tell us about the weeks, years and decades of research, writing and editing experience they bring to their work. They forget to mention the detailed planning all of them will do to write.

In the rush to become the next best-selling author on the promotional circuit, they focus instead on the finished product, and say less about the long hours of planning, researching and thinking that accompanies good writing.

Yes, there will be creative impulses, and sometimes you will not know precisely where they come from. Nonetheless, most of your best writing is underpinned by systematic organising, interpreting, critiquing and reflecting, and relies on a plan. *A writing plan.*

Some writers use yoga, others meditate, while some use dreams or relaxation to spark the writing process. Such techniques can be very useful for easing your mind and body toward the writing task.

Indeed, for some writers these techniques will become an essential part of the process. But for writing your family history, in fact any history for that matter, you will first and foremost need A PLAN.

Your writing will flow more easily, and the results will be much improved, if you plan, revise, re-read, and become more familiar with your stories early in the writing process. Your research and writing will also gain clarity and be more professional the earlier you engage with the planning process. Why let the research you have done pile up and become an uncoordinated mountain of sludge then sit down to write?

This research is important to you and is the basis of your writing—sort it out early with an appropriate outline or plan to ease yourself into the writing process.

Decisions, decisions, decisions!

Determining how you will write your family history will provide the basic stepping-off point for your writing. A pedigree or chart of the many names and dates collected can also get you started writing. These are easily assembled with a genealogical software program. Of course, the length, number and complexity of the lists make them almost unintelligible to all but the most persistent reader. Nonetheless, they are your carefully compiled and systematic record and can help you write the stories your family will enjoy reading.

One way to improve on the pedigree approach is to write about one generation at a time. This option can be limited by time (say, from the arrival of the first ancestors until their deaths), by geography (providing scope for more in-depth local history), and by name (writing only about those ancestors possessing the family name or who were members of the first arriving family). Once the first generation is completed, you can move on to the next generation as volume two of the family history.

Other approaches to writing and publication can include a simple compilation of the original research documents, arranged chronologically with attached notes and commentary linking the various sections or events together. Or, you can assemble a pictorial family history using photographs of individuals, events and places or houses as the focal point of the text. This latter approach lends itself to electronic production through video or publication on a CD/DVD.

You may choose to write biography, memoir or autobiography, use letters or diaries as a basis for your story, collate a family oral history, focus on themes or topics of interest, write from the family's occupational history or use a local or regional focus. Perhaps you will look at cooking, music, cultural difference or economic or political approaches, write fiction, or stay with the more familiar mix of personal stories, photographs, biographies and family charts. Regardless, your decision about how to write the family story and what form it will ultimately assume will essentially be one of the first steps of your writing plan.

There is no reason why you cannot be creative in choosing how to write the family history. It is your history and it is up to you to plan, create and write. A writing roadmap is the next step in making the writing task more manageable and easy.

Planning to write

A writing roadmap is a plan—you can begin with a simple list of proposed chapters, or perhaps make a list of the sections that might constitute your family story.

It is wise to begin at the beginning! Think about your family origins, move on to the first arrival in Australia, and then add in occupations and educational experiences.

The next part of the plan could list aspects of the family's changing fortunes, and their aging, then move on to the rise of new generations. A plan could also be mapped around historical periods and/or family events; the Great Depression, local floods, world wars, post-war prosperity, major family illness or death, work opportunities or changes, or a move to another place.

A writing plan will not constrain or inhibit creativity. On the contrary, it will channel your writing towards more imaginative approaches and guide you to a more positive completion of your family history.

Without some kind of roadmap for your writing, you will not know where you are going, just like when you are driving the car. And you will not know how to select, interpret and best use the documents and other information you have collected. Without some thought to planning, your writing will not do justice to the meticulous research already done.

An outline or plan could include:

- A simple list
- A writing outline
- Mapping themes
- Charting historical dates, i.e. your family in time.

You can use any of these plans or outlines to begin the writing of your family history. It might be useful to map out topics and themes at the beginning and then move on to charting historical dates as you complete more research. Any one of these plans can play a role in providing an easier pathway into organising and mapping the disparate range of material each of us collects, collates and then uses to write the family history.

A simple list

Your writing journey will improve with planning, direction, and a defined, considered approach. A simple list or a rough plan can be a list of possible chapters. Map out basic information under the chapter headings and add more detail as you move further into your writing.

As you collect more information and become more knowledgeable about the family history, your list will change. This is the challenging and exciting part of the writing journey.

Look at your proposed chapters and list relevant sources for each. Think about the stories you will include within each chapter or category, examine the time periods, and connect your family biographies to the wider historical events.

A writing outline

A basic writing outline provides the groundwork for you to look more closely and critically at your data. It will be easier to then sit down and write creatively, accurately and with a good sense of history. The following writing outline is based on a story from my mother's family history:

A Writing Outline—The Partridge Family

The basic story: Great grandfather Robert Partridge drowned in a flooded river.

Starter words and phrases: River searched, police in boat, hat found, man confused, funeral for drowned, from Sussex, England.

Sources: Newspaper report, obituary, interview with a family member.

The beginning story: Mystery Drowning—the late Mr W.R. Partridge.

The story begins when Robert Partridge left home one Friday for Kempsey where he was supposed to have planned to catch a train to Macksville (according to the newspaper report of the incident). However, the story is told differently by an elderly descendant. This informant relates that Robert Partridge frequently went to Kempsey where he would spend quite a bit of his time in a local hotel, which backed onto the Macleay River. Rather than becoming confused by the lights of Kempsey Bridge (as the press reported) and then falling into the river, it is much more likely that he was a little the worse for having partaken of the 'demon drink' and as the river was actually in flood, he probably fell in due to his state of intoxication. A constable searched along the bank after hearing cries for help but nothing was found until the next morning when Mr Partridge's hat was retrieved floating down river. The body of the drowned Partridge was found the following day. The obituary relates his age as 72, and he was survived by his wife Mary Ann and six sons and three daughters.

Originally born in Sussex, England, Robert Partridge had lived at Kinchela, where he farmed on Summer Island for many years before this untimely death.

Note how in this first draft or outline, I have used the differing versions of the story about the drowning to give depth and interest to the story.

Mapping themes

Map out topics and themes as a starting point for your roadmap. Begin your mapping with early topics such as origins, childhood, immigration, the voyage and arrival—and then move on to later periods in the family history.

In the example following, I have included some research techniques and the sources associated with each period of the family history as a guide for further research and writing.

None of these plans or guides are fixed; they are strategies to ease the writing process. Your choice of a plan or a writing approach needs to suit your writing style, your way of managing files and your understanding of the family stories.

Charting historical dates

Constructing a historical chart will give an overview, at a glance, of how your family events and their decisions to marry or travel line up against broader historical trends. With a historical chart, you can begin to visualise how the family story fits in with the framework of Australian and overseas history. See the example (on pages 114–15) I put together to chart how my family's personal history relates to the broader historical context.

Construct your own historical chart by writing down the dates, family events, countries and historical events for the period of history you are writing about, and note how your ancestors fit within the bigger picture of state, national and international history.

I have found that using a historical dictionary of Australian or other world history as a reference is a useful starting point for this chart.

Begin with well-known events and move into other periods of history more compelling and more pertinent for your family story. Mapping out historical events against the life events of characters in your family history provides a simple chart for a comparative and historical interpretation to begin your writing.

For example, I found this technique useful when writing about my great grandmother, Mary Kirkpatrick, and her experience of the First World War. Her support for this war was very different to my mother's response to the Second World War. They were both patriots but life experience gave them very different ways of responding to their immediate circumstance.

Mary Kirkpatrick, originally from Northern Ireland and staunchly British, lost her youngest son in the dying stages of the war in France. Despite this loss and general disillusionment with the conflict, she remained a firm and vocal supporter of the war and its causes. She raised money for the 'boys returning home' and looked after her son's wounded friends as they returned home.

My mother, on the other hand, married young and had her first child in mid 1939 just before the Second World War broke out. She was pregnant almost every year thereafter until

1944 just as the war was coming to an end. Poor, alone and isolated in the bush, she was also coping with what she felt was a 'bad marriage'. The war was important but it was not central to my mother's consciousness as it was for my great grandmother.

My mother and my great grandmother thus had very different views of those great world events. Their personal experiences coloured how they responded and also how they coped during these times.

The men and women in your family will also reveal similar diversity and complexity in their responses to local, national and international events. Mapping out their responses will provide rich and useful data to understand your characters' lives.

Charting your personal and family data and examining it within and through the changing prisms of the big pictures of history, provides the crucial detail to complete your plan and get you writing.

Changing the plan—it's not in the stars at all!

A plan is flexible, can change, and indeed will change and be revised again and again. This is the joy of good writing. It is a journey *you* take with your creative energies and should have no boundaries.

A roadmap or plan will change as you become more familiar with your research material and the family history, but the

Dates	England, Ireland, France	Australia	Family	Mary Kirkpatrick (G/G)	Kathleen Kyle (Mother)
1841			Kyle brothers, Henry and Michael, arrive in Sydney		
1850s	Overcrowding in London, poverty, potato famine in Ireland, increasing desperation as people turn to crime	Convict population declines, free immigrants on the rise in New South Wales	Henry Kyle m. Esther Sherlock Henry Kyle d. 1859 Esther re-marries		
1860s			She moves with children to Murwillumbah	b.1862 m.1880 Hugh Kirkpatrick Dtr Janet b. 1881. d.1882	
1870s			Young Henry Kyle leaves for Qld, m. Mary Ann Weir	First son David b. 1883 Emigrated to NSW 1884	
1880s			Mary Kirkpatrick arrives with husband and infant son	Dtr. Mary b. 1886. d. 1887	
1890s		State schools open, population growth Gold rushes, new states formed in Queensland, Victoria, South Australia	Mary Kirkpatrick leaves her husband, begins life as a single mother	Move to Armidale Second son George b. 1889 Mary leaves and begins life as a single parent 1889 Moves to Macleay Valley	
	Great Depression	Great Depression			
1900		Women gain the vote 1902	Mary Kirkpatrick, midwifery training 1902 (Sydney)	Establishes first private maternity hospital in Kempsey	
1910			1905 William Henry Kyle takes up a selection at Nulla Nulla Creek David and George Kirkpatrick take up a selection next door to Kyle's at Nulla Nulla Creek		

Year	Context	Family	Nurse Kirk	Kathleen
1914 1917	WWI	George Kirkpatrick joins the Police Force and then enlists in 1914 Wounded in July 1916, he is patched up in England, returns to France in March 1917 and is killed 15 April, 1917. 'Dave' Kirkpatrick m. Mary Partridge 1914 Lloyd George 'Georgie' b. 1915 Lorna Mary b. 1916 Nelly Jean b. 1918 My mother Kathleen b. 1919 David 'Slim Dusty' b. 1927 Georgie dies 1924	Nurse Kirk's work as a midwife is expanding George's death is devastating, she leaves Kempsey and does not return until 1924 1918 Nurse Kirk is working for the Red Cross raising funds 1919 she is working for 'our boys returning home' holding sports days to raise funds July 1920 Bellbrook candidate for Queen of the Day for the local hospital	Kathleen born 29 November 1919
1922 1937 1938	1920s prosperity 1930s Depression		Nurse Kirk returns to work 1924 Nurse Kirk retires 1937	Kathleen m. Lawrie Kyle 1937 She lives in a tent in the bush. Patricia Kathleen b. 1938, d. 1940
1939 1940 1942 1943	WWII is declared. WWII	Grandmother Kyle dies 1943	Nurse Kirk dies 1943	Shirley Margaret b. 1939 Noeline Juene b. 1940 Lance Lawrence b. 1942 Kay Francis b. 1943, c.1943
1944 1945	WWII ends. WWII ends		Dave Kirk dies 1945 Granny (Mary Partridge) leaves Nulla Nulla Creek	Phyllis b. 1944
1950s	Popular culture—music, dance and surfing—become popular with the young			1956 mother leaves and begins her life as a single parent

fact that you have a plan will focus your writing and keep you on track.

There is nothing fixed about a plan, the highways and byways and side roads can take us anywhere. A writing plan is flexible. It is a creative, dynamic and an exciting channel into your writing.

Each new sentence or paragraph you add to the mix of your writing will produce more ideas. Each time you re-read you will be surprised and delighted by the progress you make towards other ways of seeing and being as a writer.

When I first started to write the history of my great grandmother, I planned to include the stories of my mother and my sister as their lives had some similarity although lived decades apart. I could see social and economic events that were similar although occurring at very different historical times.

As I did more research on Mary Kirkpatrick's life story, however, I decided that her story was sufficient on its own. So in effect I began writing with a broader notion of what the family history would be and then narrowed to a biography.

Your plan could work in the reverse. I have seen students who begin writing focused on one character and then broaden out to write the full family history.

Keeping yourself on the writing road

A writing plan will keep your writing focused on the writing task. Even fiction writers have a plan, which they re-work and change over the time of their writing. Every doctoral student has a plan. A writing plan is a set of questions, or themes or ideas or chapters, about your story that provides a pathway for your writing.

A writing plan will get you started and keep your writing on track. The creative act of writing out your plan will energise you as well as keep you writing. It will force you to think more specifically about the writing task sooner.

Example—Writing plans

The following writing plans illustrate how a plan can be a solid starting point for early writing. The first plan was done in 1979, when I began my research; the last modification was made in the mid 1990s when I was able to find the time to write final drafts and think about publication.

Over the decades in between, I revised, re-worked and modified my plan. Although I retained basic elements of the initial plan and maintained a strong focus on women ancestors in my family, the final plan was very different to the original.

Nonetheless, working on and being able to refer to my roadmap, and using it as a template, provided a strong focus for my beginning writing. It was both an inspiration for the writing process, and a way of ensuring integrity, challenge and historical accuracy for my writing task.

Plan 1

Possible Title: Mary Kirkpatrick: Matriarch of the Macleay

Chapters: Do You Remember?; The Modern Girls; Working Women; Sisters; A Final Note.

Notes on the Storyline: The story begins with Mary (a single parent in the 1890s), traces the history of her son and his family, her granddaughter Kathleen (also a single parent in the 1950s), and my sister Shirley (a great granddaughter in the 1970s). It is a story of women coping alone, their courage, their frailties, and the common threads in their lives as well as the differences.

The story then moves on to Mary's children, especially my grandfather David and my grandmother Mary Louisa Florence Partridge. Other chapters focus on working women, within the home and outside of it. And for my sister, this is the story of a family of women, and about sisters too.

Sources/Documents: Birth, death and marriage certificates (BDMs); letters, diaries, family notes; private hospital records; nursing records; local histories; histories of health and hospitals; women's history; school records; land records; *Macleay Argus*; oral history.

Review of Previous Research: A reading of previous histories of midwifery in Australia and more generally; Australian histories; and women's history more generally.

Plan 2

Title: Memories & Dreams: A Biography of Nurse Mary Kirkpatrick

Chapter 1: The Coast   This chapter introduces the reader to the rivers, bushland and broader history of the mid north coast of New South Wales.

Chapter 2: Irish Dreams   The chapter tracing Mary Kirkpatrick's birth, childhood, growing up, marriage, and birth and death of her first child, and ending as she leaves Ireland.

Sources: Oral interviews; Belfast histories; Belfast and Ulster directories; Ballymacarrett histories; Lloyds Register of Shipping; immigration and shipping records; BDMs.

Chapter 3: The Immigrant   The early years in Sydney, birth and death of another child.

Sources: Immigration and shipping records; Pyrmont and Ultimo histories; Australian history; BDMs.

Chapter 4: A Woman Alone   Mary Kirkpatrick leaves Sydney and her feckless Irish husband, begins her Australian journey alone with her two sons.

Sources: Australian history; railway history; women's history; BDMs; letters; obituaries; histories of Armidale and Kempsey; oral interviews.

Chapter 5: Women's Business   Mary trains as a midwife then begins her lifelong work with women and babies in the Macleay Valley. The chapter also begins to tell the story of her friendships and collaboration with other local midwives.

Sources: Letters; Department of Health Reports; north coast histories; reports of the Home Training and Lying In School; Australasian Trained Nurses Association Records; *Macleay Argus*; oral interviews.

Chapter 6: Uncertain Times   An account of Nurse Kirkpatrick's early midwifery career including financial uncertainty.

Sources: Australasian Trained Nurses Association Records; *Macleay Argus*; oral interviews; family stories; *Town and Country Journal*; Histories of the Thungutti People.

Chapter 7: A Nation's Battle   My great grandmother prospers, her eldest son marries, but her youngest is killed at Lagincourt, France, and some of her dreams begin to fade.

Sources: Records of the Australian War Memorial; *Macleay Argus*; BDMs; *Macleay River Historical Society Journal*; New South Wales State Records documents; Australian histories; family stories; oral interviews; *Macleay Chronicle*.

Chapter 8: A Women's War   Nurse Kirkpatrick, devastated by her son's death, leaves midwifery to do charity work raising funds for local institutions and for the soldiers returning home.

Sources: Official war history; records of the Australian War Memorial; *Macleay Argus*; letters and diaries; local histories.

Chapter 9: Family Matters Nurse Kirkpatrick returns to midwifery, her career slows but is not over yet. She continues to work for, and with, her midwifery colleagues and friends. She is less close to her family.

Sources: Letters; oral interviews; family stories; New South Wales State Records documents; Australian histories; *Macleay Argus*; land records.

Chapter 10: In the Shadow of Mary The end of her career, and her life. The family continues, an assessment of her life, career and contribution.

Sources: Oral interviews; letters; BDMs; family stories; *Macleay Argus*.

Note that as I wrote the story, I moved towards the title concept of 'Memories' because the book is based largely on oral history and 'Dreams' because I felt my great grandmother had a dream, through immigration and hard work, to achieve prosperity and happiness in Australia.

The completed story of your family history is not fully realised until the last word is written, nor until the last plan has been drawn up!

The plan does and should change almost daily. Its construction will be the best writing start you can give yourself, and revising your plan will offer a unique opportunity for incorporating new data, understanding complex family relationships, and including the bigger themes of history much more easily and with style.

EXERCISES

- Make a plan of the historical approach you might take when writing your family history. Think about the period of history you will cover, the mix of fiction or fact you could use, and the characters that people your family history.
- Will you write a chronology, a biography, a memoir or a traditional genealogy? Why? Have you thought about how the family history will look at the end of the writing task?
- Map out topics and themes for your roadmap.
- Construct a writing outline.
- Complete your writing plan, assess where revisions might occur.

Begin your plan now

Writing is a planned activity. It is true that the creative urge to write can flow from the many emotional and professional experiences in life. It is also true that at other times you seem to write almost effortlessly, without planning and without any conscious structure or outline in mind.

But writing does come from somewhere, be it conscious or unconscious. You will write family history more easily and with more rigour if you have a plan.

Keep in mind that your plan will change. The challenge of writing well is to welcome that change and capture all of its complexity, feel empathy with it and keep on writing no matter what.

A WRITING PLAN

Begin a simple outline or plan for your family history under the following headings.

Possible title:

Possible chapters:

Sources:

Outline of the family history:

Review of previous research:

Chapter eight ✌

CHARACTERS— WHAT WOULD YOU DO WITHOUT THEM!

U sing characters to write family history can ease the writing process. Do them justice as you write about them.

Falling for your ancestors

The phenomenon of falling in love with your writing subject is not new. Even those individuals considered the worst characters, like Lenin or Hitler, receive some admiration from biographers or journalists who spend a long time researching their lives.

It is not surprising that family characters begin to loom larger than life in our imaginations and our writing. As family historians, we are writing about *real* people. We begin to believe we know them—well.

Some family historians are amused, others are amazed, by the depth of feeling they develop for particular characters. Despite, or indeed because of, our growing relationship with these characters, our writing task is made both more complex and accessible at once.

We do not really know these people, of course, but they become central to our stories, and our most passionate beliefs about the ancestral past. They become key partners in the writing of our family stories.

Compelling characters

In the past, family history has been written around *important* characters, usually men, who held prominent public positions or were sailors, soldiers or successful businessmen.

Why you find some characters more interesting than others, however, can be related to other aspects of an individual's journey through life. It is not because they are important, in the previous traditional sense, that they seem so significant now. It is more likely to be because you have developed an emotional attachment to them.

There is no doubt you begin to like these characters a lot as you learn more about their struggles and achievements through their lifetimes. You are proud of these characters, you want to see how their lives can be compared or linked to your own, and you want to know as much as possible about them.

As a family historian, you need characters. They are the lifeblood of your many stories, and your feelings about them will motivate and stimulate you with your research and writing.

Characters can be an entry point—an important, invigorating and compelling entry point—for writing the family history. The question is: how do you write about them well?

Complex people

Typically in family history, we tend to fall into the trap of writing about mothers as angels or stepfathers as villains. I have done this myself. Writing about the second marriage of my father's great grandmother, I recorded a story of how the new stepfather was a harsh disciplinarian. The family story continues that this overly harsh parenting caused my father's grandfather, Henry 'Harry' Kyle, to leave as soon as he could. The story fits with the later life of this character, recalled by his children and grandchildren as 'wilder', tougher and lived well away from his mother, stepfather, siblings and half-siblings.

I do, however, need to be cautious in how I interpret such events, as I cannot know exactly the events that led young Harry to leave his family. It is possible there was some friction between Harry and his stepfather, as he was the only one to leave the family home. However, to attribute fault or some kind of wicked intent on the part of the stepfather without evidence would be unfair and unconvincing from this long view of history.

I like the approach that author L.P. Gouldrup takes to writing about characters. He suggests that characters will have *consistent* personality traits that will follow them through their lifetime, although they will undergo some change as they age.

For characters to be historically accurate and believable, they should have a mixture of good and bad qualities. Real people move between admirable and less than admirable qualities throughout their lives. This mixture of good and bad character traits can be placed under *complexity* of character. In addition, most characters are predictable in their personality and these attributes are placed under *consistency* of character.[1]

In general, the changes a character will display are less about personality and more about external factors (i.e. they might learn not to play the stock market and lose, but take a bad temper to their grave). They may become sadder, wiser, perhaps more at peace, as they age; but their basic personality traits will remain in place.

Therefore, the characters you meet in the pages of your family history are not one-dimensional. They are complex, contradictory, even contrary. Look for the many-sided aspects of your characters, seek out their faults as well as their good points.

Gouldrup offers the following example of a 'too good to be real' character in writing family history:

Elisa May Manwaring was a woman with strong courage, great determination and complete faith in God and His goodness. All of these virtues were wrapped with a happy disposition and a very ready laugh. She had many friends who loved her dearly. Her family would have done almost anything to make her happy but she was so independent that she seldom asked for help. Rather, she turned to help others in her most trying hours.[2]

Against this too positive portrayal, compare the following excerpt from 'Never in a Month of Sundays', by Lybbie Semple, which paints a more realistic picture of the characters in a mother/daughter relationship:

I am a *Mother* of three; step*Mother* of two and I have my own *Mother*. She is ninety-one. A little slower but still going strong. Still able to pull strings that can turn my life upside down. A word here. A look there. A sign. A half asked question that tests the waters, waters of guilt or remorse in which I am already up to my armpits. Now she is frail, somewhat stubborn, and I find myself becoming the *mother's Mother*, 'taking over' or supervising my mother in situations which ten years ago she would have acted upon without hesitation. This daughter/mother role is different for not only does it involve two adults but two adults with an interconnected life history spanning more than fifty-three years. A history which often has to be put aside to enable the two of us, the elder one now in need of care, to go about our daily lives in freedom from *olde worlde* baggage. I find myself my mother's confessor and I endeavour to step back and listen with the ears and heart of a good friend, neither judging nor condemning. The letting go of my mother, I can only imagine at this stage, will be one of the most difficult challenges of faith and love I will have had to face.[3]

To paint your characters well, write about mothers, grandmothers and great grandmothers as women who meet the challenges of mothering as best they can. Write about fathers, stepfathers, grandfathers and great grandfathers, not as stereotypes who do not seem to have any complexity or contradiction in their personality, but as characters who have diverse attitudes, wits, hopes and dreams, demanding and different lifestyles, and complicated relationships.

Characters open a window to easier writing

It is true that you do not know people in your past. However, they begin to have a presence in your research, anyway. They were once real, they lived a full life, and you want to write as fully as you can about them.

One way of doing this is to think about your character's life journey and capture it in your writing. Your characters were born, were children, grew up, married, built homes, farmed, took care of family, worked and then aged.

You are fortunate if your parents or grandparents told endless stories and someone listened and wrote them down. You will be pleased if there are letters, obituaries, press reports, diaries or other treasured family artefacts that can fill out the picture of how individual characters lived their lives.

Characters do open windows to easier writing. They provide colour, description, adventure and humour, and lead you to look more closely at relationships within the family.

I found my great grandmother's history in the same landscape where I grew up and I did feel a personal and emotional connection to that family history. My great grandmother and my mother were both single parents, although at very different times in history; my great grandmother in the 1890s and my mother in the 1950s. The common social and economic struggles experienced by my mother and my great grandmother provide powerful emotional triggers for some of my writing of the Kirkpatrick family history.

What did they say?

Introducing dialogue into your writing of the family history is acceptable so long as your reader is aware that the words you give your characters are drawn from memory and imagination or from interviews. Readers should be told the words being used to create the dialogue are not precise and are not what actually took place.

> Memory is faulty, we rehearse our stories, add to them, embellish them, indeed we often sanitise them and, within the family, the re-telling can change and shape the original story into a more compelling, adventurous or heroic tale.

Writers of memoir who use considerable dialogue in their text are asked how did they remember it so well. Some reply that they have a good memory. No doubt this is true of some writers. Most do acknowledge, however, that the dialogue is largely made up, albeit that it is based on reminiscence of parents or grandparents and conversations, over the years, with family members.

Perhaps you would like to include dialogue based on stories your parents or grandparents have told you. It is important to get these stories onto the page and to write them exactly as you hear them. However, the words are not precise and are not what actually took place. So how do we sort out the 'fiction' from fact?

Your reader should be told when something is 'true' and when something is not. Writing a memoir is different to writing family history. In researching and writing history, you should aim to seek truth, accuracy and authenticity in your construction of the past. You cannot make it up. If you 'invent' dialogue then it is fiction and not history.

It is possible, however, to use dialogue, or reconstruct conversations, or use anecdotes in your writing, to enliven significant events, re-create important scenes, or simply to bring your characters and their lives into sharper focus.

Dialogue is the most useful device the novelist has to provide the reader with a picture of a character's emotions, attitudes, ideas, thoughts and feelings. I have also read oral histories, autobiographies, memoirs and local histories where dialogue is included, sometimes successfully, sometimes not.

Using anecdote

For those interested in introducing dialogue into the family history, the employment of conversation and anecdote can be helpful. This is not the same thing as using a verbatim quote from a letter, a court case or an oral history.

An anecdote is something that is remembered by a person or persons and then narrated to others. Within families, anecdotes, especially about interesting characters, are well known and lovingly re-told. They are compelling parts of the life journey of mothers, fathers, aunts, uncles, grandparents and children being passed down over several generations.

Using anecdote is common in family history and an excellent device to provide a unique flavour to the story. For example, this anecdote was included in *Memories & Dreams*. It was told to me by Joe Dodds, the young man referred to in the story:

In 1935 and 1936, Joe Dodds delivered medicines to all of the hospitals in Kempsey and he relates that Nurse Kirk was still at Kirkwood (Private Hospital), possibly helping out with the supervision of nursing staff and providing back-up support and advice. Joe recalls that if he was a bit too long arriving with the medicines—he had to ride a bicycle after waiting for them to be made up at Lane's Pharmacy—Nurse Kirk would be very testy with him. As a lad of fifteen, Joe found her a very fierce and imposing woman. Nurse Kirk was by this time in her mid seventies. He did remember a more tolerant and gentler person as Nurse Kirk would play records on her gramophone for him knowing that he loved music. Joe Dodds went on to establish and play in many local bands in the 1950s and 1960s.[4]

Re-creating conversations

Another way of working with dialogue in family history is to write about re-creating conversations. Re-creating conversation relates to how characters did talk. We can write about accents, whether characters talked slowly or very quickly, or whether they seemed nervous. Or, maybe they mumbled or had a stutter. Perhaps your ancestor was articulate for the times, or they may have had an educated way of talking. You do not have to remember conversations word for word and, indeed, you cannot if you are writing about ancestors from long ago.

For example, you might write something like the following:

Aunt Lorna could not remember exactly the words she heard that day. But she insisted the family knew exactly what their father decided that morning. 'I'll sell the whole farm or none of it,' he said.

Just these few words spoken by the father adds drama to the story. We want to know more about his decision and how it affected the family.

Alternatively, the remembered conversation can be more extensive as in the following excerpt from 'She Had a Wicked Wit,' by Jan Gracie Mulcahy, where a daughter is writing about her mother and her battle with Alzheimers. In the recorded conversation, it is clear that, although her mother has a fading memory, her mother's personality and wit are still well and truly in play:

A few days later I visit Mum in the morning. She is lying propped up on pillows in a half sitting position looking surprisingly well groomed. Her colour is very good and her cheeks nicely puffed out with teeth in place. All those tiny facial wrinkles have disappeared entirely. However she is being jostled and bounced about while two attendants attempt to attach some iron railings to her bed and her mood is not good. One man looks Asian and the other seems to be Greek. They are having some serious communication problems and Mum's angry comments do not help.

'Incompetent fools! What are they trying to do?' She asks. I attempt to explain the men are fitting safety railings to the bed to prevent her falling out at night.

'I don't want a safety railing. I have never fallen out of bed. Here, take these,' and with that, she spits out her teeth onto her chin where they protrude like a false, wet grin.

I swoop on the teeth and whip them out of sight with a tissue.

'They drive me mad,' she complained. 'They don't fit. They must be someone else's.'

I disappear to the bathroom and wash the teeth feeling helpless and stupid.

My thoughts are desperate. Why can't they remove her from the bed and then fix it? Why didn't she just die during that last stroke? No, no, I must not think those thoughts.

It is bedlam in the bedroom after I return. It seems full of people; three bed-ridden patients, two nurses hovering around a trolley, a radio blaring and the Greek and Asian chaps now on their knees, cranking and clunking at the railing on Mum's bed.

'What are they doing now? Praying,' she observes, 'it won't do any good. Never does.'

One of the young nurses giggled uncomfortably as Mum looks at me furiously.

'I tell you my girl, when you reach this stage . . . well, quite frankly, I'd rather be dead.'

I gasp. How like her to come right out with the unspeakable.

'I'll see if they can put the railing on later and give you some peace Mum.'

I leave the room to find the Sister-in-Charge, and ask for the railing to be attached while Mum is out patrolling the corridors. When I return to the bedroom, Mum has dropped off to sleep and the attendants are nowhere to be seen. The railing lies on the floor.

That evening when I called in to check on Mum, the railing was still not fitted to the bed and I don't know whether that was because the attendants had given up or my instructions to the Sister had been carried out.

And the teeth? Well, that was the last time Mum ever wore them. After that day they kept company with their little box, the toothbrush, caramels, white hairs, broken chocolates and various other assorted odds and ends which gave a personal stamp to my eccentric mother's top drawer.[5]

The fortunate life syndrome

In family history, you can fall very quickly into the trap of stereotyping your characters. Quoting from parents and grandparents, you write a sentimental and nostalgic view of childhood, parenting and family relationships.

For example: 'My father/mother/grandmother/grandfather had a heart of gold.' Or: 'Those were beautiful days when we were all so happy.'

If you think only in these stereotypical or clichéd forms then your characters and their family events will not be authentic. If you use only clichés or stereotypes for describing your ancestors, your family history will be weighed down with undue sentimentality and one-dimensional characterisation.

Instead, write about your characters as *real* people. There are some basic techniques for listing family, personal and community facets that can describe characters more fully. Author and family historian Charley Kemphorne has the following techniques for making characters real in family history:

1. Describe physical reality (looks, mannerisms, or overall impressions you find in your research).
2. Use dialogue.
3. Show how the characters acted or reacted to everyday things. We can all relate a story about how our mothers or grandmothers were forever cleaning or tidying up. Or we remember how our fathers or grandfathers filled, packed and generally enjoyed the ritual of smoking a pipe.

What did other people (neighbours, work colleagues, extended family) think about your character/s? This information can come from interviews, or letters, or newspaper reports. Obituaries can also provide clues about the character of individuals.[6]

Characters are not fiction

In fiction, characters are not the same as people. If you are writing a novel, you will be told to make your characters larger than life, or composites of several people. Real people, you will be told, are boring.

But in history, real people are what we have to write about and they are not fictional. And they cannot be made up. In addition, as noted earlier, real characters have a blend of weaknesses as well as strengths.

Real people were stubborn, narrow-minded, often harsh, even unlikeable.

Real people were hardworking but they could also be tired, depressed, lonely and uncertain.

Real people had conflict in their lives. They were inevitably caught up in family quarrels and misunderstandings with brothers, fathers, mothers, children, sisters, aunts and neighbours. Most of us can find stories about disagreement and conflict within the family. Those disagreements, family friction and antagonism will provide clues about individual character and ideas for writing about them.

Getting to know your characters

Why not construct a fact file on your characters? Creating a file of interesting facts can be a useful technique to get to know characters and write more skilfully and knowledgeably about them.

A fact file is not the same as writing a biography or a story. It is a relatively easy task to construct a biography or a story about a character closer to us in history. It is more difficult when that person lived in the seventeenth, eighteenth or nineteenth century.

A fact file is a way of organising your research information so as to write more accurately and perhaps with more interest about a character.

Wedding photographs are the most commonly surviving images in family records, and can be scrutinised for valuable information about clothing, hairstyles, jewellery, and facial shape and expression. The shape of noses, colour of eyes and general demeanour will help with description. Family stories, legends and myths can also provide clues to character, family relationships and how individuals coped from time to time.

For example, my aunts and uncles have told me a story about their grandmother, Mary Ann Kyle, who had 'sparkling blue eyes'; this description lending some weight to other perceptions I had about her. She died when I was three and I do not remember her at all but, according to family stories, she seems to have shown tenacity, strength of character, toughness and resilience in the face of a marriage to a rather wild, rough and ready bushman. The 'sparkling blue eyes' story reminds me of this as I continue to write.

Examine education and work records for the small pieces of data that can provide clues to building a character file. Australian education records are very good. If the enrolment and/or punishment records survive for that small school your parents, grandparents and uncles and aunts attended, you will find useful information on appearance, character and family relationships.

Think about other aspects of character development, such as motivation and family conflict. We write at length about our ancestor's desire to achieve prosperity, land, and significant wealth, education and work opportunities, but we focus less on other characteristics such as politics, philanthropy or discrimination, or issues of race, class or gender.

Examine what people read. Did your grandparents read local or overseas newspapers? Ask the family about their reading and what influenced them to choose or keep certain books. It is difficult to determine reading habits of characters we know little about. If you do not know, look at the popular fiction, newspapers and arts, such as film, stage performance and dance, of the time and reflect on how these may have been part of your character's life.

The website <http://www.genealogy.com/bio/index/html> offers a free-to-download list of writing ideas titled 'Biography Assistant'. Although this list is US-centric, it does provide a range of topics and questions useful to round out the data in a character fact file, including:

Birth/adoption	Gender issues
Death and losing loved ones	Holidays
Discrimination and issues of race	Immigration
Demonstrations and protests	Marriage
Divorce	Medical history
Education	Occupation
Entertainment	Personal finances
Family relations	Personality and values
Family traditions	Physical characteristics
Friendships	Religion[7]

Similarly, under the heading 'Character Dossier', Hazel Edwards in *Writing a 'Non-boring' Family History* lists topics—such as name, age span, appearance, hair, eyes, clothes, job or skills, motivations, hobbies, strengths, weaknesses, friends, family, partner, children, adversaries/competitors/enemies, aspirations and greatest problems[8]—for family historians to use and include in their character descriptions as an aid to constructing the character fact file.

It is difficult to write well about characters we know little about, especially those ancestors from the long past. Imagination, interpretation and speculation can help your writing here, although keep in mind that when you write imaginatively you must inform the reader.

In *Memories & Dreams* I used some imagination, interpretation and speculation to write about Mary Kirkpatrick's childhood:

Mary was tall as an adult, lanky, a little testy, hard to please sometimes. As the eldest child in the family, did she toss her thick, fair hair behind her running along Ormeau Road taunting other children to keep up, as if they could? I can imagine she lifted her books easily, walking swiftly to school gathering Margaret, her young sister, her small brothers James and George behind her, already taking care. On Sundays Mary would have helped her mother dress the younger children ready for church. They would have walked down Albert Bridge Road, the smokestacks in the distance and the sounds of the ships stowed in the harbour never far away. The Magees, and the Kirkpatricks, the family Mary married into, were well-known supporters of the Orange Orders, with their complicated history, their Protestant faith and their politics tightly held. These family names are still strongly associated with Protestant politics and religious intolerance in Northern Ireland.[9]

I have used facts well known about Mary Kirkpatrick, such as her place in the family (as the eldest child), her height (she was tall), her gender and temperament (a little forbidding at times but professional, articulate, straightforward), to create a template for reflecting on her childhood.

I also looked at specific local history published about the streets of Belfast and the politics and economics of the time, as well as ideas on family relationships (for example, as the eldest daughter Mary would have helped her mother with the childcare and other domestic chores), to construct this text. I also used information from family stories and photographs about her hair colour (thick, blond and wavy), her possible maturity and caring for her age (she became a trained and professional midwife in Australia, cared deeply for her family and was involved in the community), and also the political dimensions of her childhood, to write about a child I had little knowledge about.

You, too, can use facts gleaned from birth, death and marriage certificates, from local histories and stories or myths in the family, to write about characters in the long past or a childhood you know little about.

Are you a character too?

The most difficult question faced in writing about characters is writing yourself into the story. I find family historians are confused about their role as a writer, as a narrator of the family stories and also as a character in the text.

At times I find the author is 'I' and Jane Smith all on the one page. And Jane Smith, having written a perfectly interesting and credible family history about origins, immigration and new lives, suddenly begins writing something like:

> Jane said her mother Martha Smith (nee Hope) told the story that, as a child when she went to town, she would... Jane spoke with other grandchildren and family friends during the course of her research and gleaned more detailed information about her grandmother.

It would be less clumsy and quite acceptable to rewrite this as:

> My mother Martha Smith (nee Hope) told me the story
> that, as a child when she went to town, she would... I
> spoke to other grandchildren and family friends during the
> course of my research and gleaned more detailed information
> about my grandmother.

Having grown up reading traditional history that rarely gave me a glimpse of the author, I am very aware of how difficult it is to 'write yourself in' to the family history. However, using 'I' or 'my' will add to your story. It will also facilitate your ability to introduce some of the writing strategies offered in this book such as 'writing about your research journey'. In addition, your readers will want to know about you as the person writing the family history. See the following sections especially 'the intrusive narrator' for more information on how best to include yourself appropriately in the written text.

Point of view

I am asked about point of view often, and it is a topic that generates considerable confusion. There are many books on point of view for fiction writers but it is not a topic well covered for history. It is a topic, however, most family historians will need to address. In family history, the following point of view choices are the most common:

- First person
- Second person
- Third person, limited and omniscient
- Intrusive narrator.

First person

This point of view is used in autobiography and memoir, and has become popular in fiction. It is the first choice for creative non-fiction, personal journey writing and stream of consciousness approaches, and plays a role in some newspaper articles. For example, if writing in the first person in the present tense:

> So here I am stuck here in Tokyo for two days. I have a single room until Denis arrives from Europe. Tomorrow I will contact Mrs Yo and begin my search of the Yokomo district.

If writing in the first person in the past tense:

> So there I was stuck in Tokyo for two days. I had a single room as Denis was in Europe. On the first day I contacted Mrs Yo and began a search of the Yokomo district.

The first-person point of view is not used often in history or family history, and it is difficult to do so successfully.

Second person

The second-person point of view is hard to sustain for long periods. In second person, rather than 'I', the narrator or writer becomes 'you'. As in:

> Turning the corner you hear the first warnings of discord.

The use of second person point of view is more suited to other genres of writing, such as self-help, and is not recommended for family history as it can be awkward and constrictive.

Third person, limited

The most common point of view in history and family history is third-person limited. In this approach the writer does not enter the mind of the characters, but can move freely, in the story, over time and place.

This approach is preferred by traditional historians who believe history writing should be confined to what they can legitimately and historically verify. For example:

> Parkes had handed on the federal 'leadership' to Edmund Barton, a Sydney barrister and protectionist politician.[10]

Or in this example by J.F.C. Harrison:

When Lovett and his fellow radicals talked of respectability and improvement, they used the same words as their middle-class contemporaries, but their meaning was different.[11]

Third person, omniscient

With this point of view, the writer does enter the mind of the character and is able to write as though they are the character as well as the author. This approach is used in creative non-fiction, but is not popular in family history. Lawrence Gouldrup gives the following example of a family history written in third-person omniscient:

When Henry reached his rooms at the top of the stairs above the tavern . . . he was surprised to find his wife packing all they owned in a large wooden crate.[12]

Another example is from Sherri Szeman's *Mastering Point of View*:

Hunching his shoulders against the cold, pelting rain, Major MacTraven slipped a hand under his caped coat to assure himself his spare pistol remained in position. A sudden gust of wind rattled rain up his campaign hat and spattered his face and hands. Desperately tired and carrying the gnawing hunger from three missed meals, he glanced back along the road at the scattered travelers.[13]

Intrusive narrator

Introducing yourself as the 'I' in the family history, that is, becoming a commentator on the stories, the characters and the events in the writing, can have limitations for the family historian. Because the material you are dealing with in the family history can be tragic, or sad, or touching, there is a tendency for you, as the 'I' in the story, to be overwhelmed by the emotions. And as you write yourself into the action, there is a danger that you will fall prey to sentimentality and oversimplification.

Very few of us can be as brutal as the novelist or memoirist, who argue that total honesty and a measure of ruthlessness (with the way you portray other people's lives) is necessary for good writing.

In addition, the people (i.e. your relatives) will be defined in relation to you—it will be your grandma; it will be Aunt Jane instead of Jane Brown, daughter of Tom Brown. There is nothing wrong with this as this is your story and you may tell it any way that appeals to you.

Including your research journey as part of the family history does require that you become an intrusive narrator and is one of the more useful methods of employing 'I' in the text. For example, writing about Mary Wollstonecraft in Paris during the French revolution, Richard Holmes writes:

What were Mary Wollstonecraft's initial impressions of Paris, the first liberated city of Europe? I expected a paean of praise and excitement; a wild traveller's letter full of the crowds, the Federe soldiers, the tricolour flags and the wall-posters, impressions of the cafes and arcades, and news of the Convention ... It gradually dawned on me that Mary, for all her genuine revolutionary enthusiasm, was frightened and isolated; but being Mary, she was not going to show it — at least to her sister.[14]

Choosing a point of view

Most family history, and indeed most history, is written from the third-person point of view. As in:

If Nurse Kirk had travelled to Ireland she would have found a different Belfast to when she left in 1884, one with significant social and economic change.

And increasingly we add in the 'I', that is, we place ourselves in the text. For example:

My great grandmother never travelled although I had thought once that she could easily have afforded it. Travel, too, might have lifted her eyes away from some of the bad times.

In choosing a point of view, ask the following questions:

1. How will you, as the writer, refer to people? Will it be Great-grandfather William, or Billy, or just William or William Henry ... ?

2. If most or even only two of the women in the family are called Mary, or are all Elizabeth, or are all Marianne or Anne, how will you refer to them, especially when you might be writing about them on the same page? Will you refer to them by their maiden names? By their married names? I had this problem as my grandmother and great grandmother were both named Mary Kirkpatrick. In order to separate them, I referred to my grandmother as Mary (Partridge), using her maiden name, and to my great grandmother as Mary Kirkpatrick.

3. As the writer of the family history, will you have a presence or a position to take in the story? Will you make comments on the research journey or on significant events?

Example

The following excerpt is from 'She was Delicate but Strong, like a Bone China Cup' by Hazel Holmes:

A small woman stood at the rail of the ship peering down at the wharf below. Her head-hugging hat hid most of her curly brown hair but did nothing to shelter her lovely English skin. Her short, twenties dress echoed the times and showed off her slim figure. Her expression showed both anxiety and a little fear. Suddenly, her face broke into a lovely smile. She had seen her brother waving from the wharf below. After leaving England on 19 June 1923 her journey was over and she had arrived safely in Brisbane. It was now 25 September 1923 ...[15]

Hazel Holmes writes about her mother's life in England and Australia with love and compassion, and traces her mother's journey through a long and sometimes difficult marriage, hard work, and an active and interesting older age. The author ends her story:

Although her family did not expect Mum to 'make old bones', because they mistakenly thought she was delicate, she proved to be like the bone china cup my youngest son likened her to, deceptively delicate but strong in both body and character. She lived to be eighty-four. Life had been hard for Mum and she had many disappointments, she nearly always showed a happy face and her strength of character carried her through a not-so-perfect life.[16]

EXERCISES

- Is there a character in your family history you 'like' more than the others? Perhaps it is a great grandmother whose life story appeals or maybe it is a mysterious seafaring great uncle? Where did you meet your favourite character? (Of course you cannot always meet them in person. The question refers to where in your research did you meet them.) Write about that meeting and what it meant to you. Why do you like them so much? How do you explain your emotional attachment to this character?

- Choose a photograph from your family collection, study it and ask the following:
  - Are there specific memories associated with the photograph?
  - Are there anecdotes?
  - Does it bring a family story to mind?
  - Is there a significant character in the photograph? What is the history of the people in it?
  - When was the photograph taken? What was the event?
  - What historical questions does the photograph pose?
  - If you placed this photograph in a book, what would the caption be? What would it be illustrating?
- Having trouble writing about your character? Try the reconstruction strategy. With this strategy, you reconstruct as many of the lives of the men and women associated with your ancestor as you can. By looking at the lives of brothers, sisters, father and mother, husband or wife, sons, daughters, friends of the family, business partners or neighbours, you will hopefully stumble across some additional information about your ancestor.

There would be no history without characters

There might be a history written somewhere that does not mention the contribution of people although I cannot imagine it. All history is created because people are born, grow up, marry and work. History is about how individuals and groups contribute to the economy, are political or not, are in business or are workers, sail across worlds to gain money, power or land, are rich or poor, try to change ideas or devote their lives toward the betterment of others. Without people we cannot know why a family is the way it is—and through the lives of characters we begin to build that bigger picture about the family. Use your characters, be passionate about them but also be critical, too.

Chapter nine ↶

NOSTALGIA, SENTIMENT AND BLAZING SUNSETS

Too sentimental, too romantic, too ready to overstate? Learn how to use passion and nostalgia to write your family stories well.

Using nostalgia and sentiment

Nostalgia and sentiment! These two words are anathema, a scourge—for professional historians.

How many times have you heard the criticisms of family history: that it is too sentimental, too romantic, and pedestrian. The critics tell you that family historians simply take a nostalgic journey into the past. Step back, you are told, and become more critical, like them!

For family historians, however, nostalgia and sentiment are the dynamic forces and the emotional core for writing family history.

How can you avoid nostalgia and sentiment in family history? Nostalgia lives in the same space as memory. It is there when you talk to older relatives, or when you think about the family. It is part of that emotional bond you feel as you meet and admire the characters in your stories.

There is no doubt there are benefits for the writer here. You can use the passion and emotional drive you find in that nostalgic journey to write more vividly and truthfully about the past. It is that passion that will inspire you as you meet the landscape, the music, the myths, the sounds and the stories of family history. You will write more easily and with greater honesty if you do allow that passion to be part of your research and writing.

Use your memories

The memories in your family history are the most important asset you have for your writing. Are they emotional? Yes. Are they nostalgic? Yes. Are they passionate? Of course.

Memories are a complex amalgam of myth, legend, fact, hope, dreams, and a long period of telling and re-telling in the family. By the time you get to write, many memories will be forgotten. Hopefully enough remain to colour your writing and to ease your pathway between pen and page.

Memories are sometimes all you have to fill out the lives of characters and add flair to your writing. Your interviews with family members are too valuable to dismiss as nostalgia.

So, although you will need to be critical and examine everything you use and draw on for your writing, always place a high value on family memory. Some reminisces may simply be 'tall tales' embellished and layered with half-truths through time and many tellers. Others will provide the tiny pieces of gold to fill in gaps, to describe characters, or to open a window into further research and writing.

It is your job as a historian to sort out the wheat from the chaff. There are traps for the unwary and the uncritical, of course. Meeting nostalgia and sentiment head on is a good rule of thumb in family history, but keep a critical and keen eye open so that your writing remains professional, pithy and precise.

Keep it real

Of course, there are limits. Do not let your passionate need to draw on nostalgia and sentiment become a barrier to writing well. By all means collect all of the stories you can. Use them wisely to shape your family history, to enhance it and finally to make it a professional historical piece.

When writing, try to avoid personalising your analysis by using words such as 'we', 'our country', and 'in our culture'. Australian history, like all others, varies enormously over time and place, and it is best to respect that variety in formal prose. The following text illustrates the problem well:

As we read our family history, we should perhaps try to relate to it by comparing how we live now, more than 100 years later... These days we have our modern transport, our comfortable homes... Our pioneering ancestors in this country had none of the everyday facilities and home comfort that we take for granted.

The 'we' and the 'our' in this writing assumes that these specific lives and their history reflect Australian history as well. This is an erroneous assumption. Whose modern transport is the author talking about here? Whose comfortable lives? Certainly, it would not be Indigenous Australians. Nor could these references be applied equally to all Australians today.

The personalising of headings and subheadings in a family history rarely works well. Use generic headings rather than terms like 'James's mother and ancestors' or 'Jane's father and ancestors' as these are confusing for the reader. Stay with headings that contain the name of the family or person being written about, for example. 'James Brown and family' or Jane Smith and family'.

Creative writing

Writing family history is a creative activity. Do not be afraid to open and read the pages of creative writing books or to attend creative writing classes. But that is for fiction writers,

I hear you say! Family history is not fiction! That is true. However, family history is full of gaps and there is no way we can know its detail exactly.

Creative strategies, including the use of imagination and interpretation, will always be part of the family history writing process. You will find strategies to help you do this throughout this book. It is important to remember that history is not fiction, however, and the fictional devices you do use are chosen to support your history and not to override it.

The senses

It will be so much easier for you to write about your great grandmother or earlier ancestors if you think about the detail of their lives more thoughtfully and creatively. By all means add in emotion, feelings and passion, and do not forget the senses: smell, sight, taste, touch and hearing.

Telling the reader how something tasted, or about the smell, or what it looked like, will add to the clarity of your stories, and it will add a more specific quality to your writing.

Using the senses adds to the reader's enjoyment. The reader can almost feel they are there in the story with the text—the story becomes more real as the reader imagines they, too, can touch, feel and taste the moments described.

Show the reader—through feelings, emotion, family stories, perceptions, ideas and more specific details. For example, rather than an uninteresting description of grandmother's brown federation house somewhere in a large city, you could write the following:

> Grandmother Smith spoke of her love of this old house. I have seen it since and it looks dark and gloomy but it was a substantial house for those times. I have been told there were olive green curtains at the front windows and the garden was awash with bright flowers when the Smith family lived there in 1896. My grandmother was a keen gardener, and the smell of roses and the jasmine she planted under her bedroom window are remembered still.

Show don't tell

There are many 'rules' of creative writing for fiction and non-fiction writers, but the homily 'show don't tell' is perhaps the most well known. It is useful advice for the writer of family history.

In family history there is a tendency for wordy, overlong and unfortunately quite boring descriptions of places and people. In other words, too much telling!

How many times do we need to read that the road was long, the journey hard or the household busy, or unedifying descriptions of a respectable, hardworking family.

It may well be that all of these generalisations are true about your family, as they are about mine and as they are about your neighbour's. What you have to do when writing is to show the reader why, where or how your family had a hard journey; you have to show how, why and when the household was busy; or how that person or that family was respectable and hardworking.

The following example is a wordy, abstract reference to Uncle Henry:

If it were not for the strong family support system which instilled in Uncle Henry strong family values and morals, he would not have succeeded so well in his life.

The example above is generalised and uninteresting to read. Using more concrete details this rewritten piece evokes vivid images, thus 'showing' the reader Uncle Henry's family values and circumstances.

Although Uncle Henry's mother did not have a car or running water, the family still lived more comfortably than did other families they knew. He learned early on that his mother made the most of what little she had, and she was known and respected for her generosity.

Here is another example of an abstract, generalised and overstated description:

My mother was a nice woman, always helpful, never harsh
or difficult. She was generous, happy and friendly. She liked
to visit friends and family.

Instead of this vague, simplified description, try to be more
specific and tease out what the terms actually mean, or add
in other details that explain characters and events in more
concrete ways. For example:

My mother helped her neighbours often, taking food or
clothing to families in need. She also shared books, wool
and knitting and sewing patterns with friends. I can remember
a day when we children were all bundled into the pony
trap and off we set for Aunt Julie's place more than ten
miles away. Aunt Julie seemed to be unwell a lot. Later I
found out she died with pulmonary disease when I was eight.

Too many blazing sunsets

Beginning writers can be carried away with show AND tell—
where there is too much detail and far too much emotional
baggage peppering the prose.

With fiction writers this can be found in the many 'blazing
sunsets' described where colour and the 'rosy fingers of dusk'
begin to overtake the writing. You do need description, but
not too much or so much that it overwhelms the text.

Next time you are reading a novel, how do you react when the story moves into a long description? Are you impatient to get back to the dramatic aspects of the story, especially back to the dialogue and the events surrounding the characters? Too much description slows the story (and your reading), and this is the case for family history writing too.

In family history the 'blazing sunsets' syndrome appears when you use too many adjectives and adverbs instead of staying with simple, straightforward prose. In family history there is much use of words like colossal, absolutely, fabulous and mighty. We find overused adjectives like terrific, huge, extraordinary, great, fantastic, massive and nice.

In addition I read phrases and words such as very, always, also, sadly (as in 'sadly he died' or 'sadly passed on' or 'sadly seven of the children died') often in family history.

It is your job as a family historian to look for the right words to use in describing or explaining your characters and the events of their lives. Do not be tempted by lazy alternatives. Stay away from the 'blazing sunsets' of too many unnecessary adjectives and adverbs, and the undue influence of the 'rosy fingers of dusk'.

Too much abstraction is a distraction

Clarity of language reveals clarity of thought—stay with the concrete, the clear and the concise in your writing. Do not assume the reader will know what you are talking about irrespective of the words used. The reader will not know unless you avoid all possible ambiguity. The meanings of every word and phrase should be crystal clear; if they are not, you have not explained yourself in a straightforward, concise way.

Stay with the concrete rather than the abstract when writing, or at least try to balance the two. For example, to write something like 'She saw the house in the distance?' is not very interesting for the reader.

From this short abstract sentence, you can imagine a house of some kind in the distance but that is about all. Is it a hut, a large house or a cottage, or so far away that you can only begin to see the shape as you draw near to it? Will there be a smudge of smoke rising from the chimney? Is it located in a small garden, or a large paddock, or squashed into the greyness of a suburban landscape.

Substituting another word for house, like hut, mansion, cottage, hovel, shed or terrace, provides greater scope for the reader's imagination. The use of specific wording is helpful for the reader, and adds to the colour and texture of your writing.

Be specific rather than vague when writing family history. Avoid using words like 'our country' or 'our culture' as culture, history and family vary greatly over time and place. Vague overgeneralised terms, such as 'the people', or 'the masses', add nothing to the reader's understanding of your family history. Be aware of the diversity of people's lives in the past, and write more professionally and with greater ease.

Formal versus informal

Traditionally, history has been written in a formal style but more recently it has moved to include informal techniques. Contrast the following examples; the first published in 1974, the second in 1982, and the last in 1999:

> Australia was conceived officially when King George III announced to parliament on 22 January 1787 that a plan had been made to 'remove the inconvenience which arose from the crowded state of the gaols in the different parts of the kingdom'.[1]

> Oral history in Australia is not only alive and well, it is kicking, and that is not a claim that can be readily made for most other branches of history.[2]

> I have known of the Mayne inheritance since I was a child. My knowledge probably dates from the late 1920s when Mary Emelia and James Mayne, the last of the family, donated the money to buy the St Lucia site for the University of Queensland.[3]

Most family history will be a mix of formal and informal styles. The more relaxed approach to history and other non-fiction more common today, can be used in your writing. Your preference for subject matter, the writing style you adopt and the historical approach you choose is up to you.

Eulogising family history

Unfortunately, much family history is not lean, mean and to the point but long, overwritten and poorly presented. Too much emotion and uncritical commentary can mar the writing.

Published family history leans towards the verbose. There are great stories published with compelling text but there is also too much extravagant language. Often the reader is left wondering if they are reading an eulogy, an angry diatribe or a list of individual achievements, instead of a family history.

We read about devoted wives, hardworking men, dear children and pious daughters. When you read words like these that describe characters in excessive terms—either as very, very good, or very, very bad—your internal antennae should go up.

Perhaps these descriptions will turn out to be perfectly valid—you may find murderers, lunatics, criminals, convicts or madwomen among your ancestry. However, the majority of women and men in your family history will not be like that. They will be like you, like your mother, like your grandmother. They will be complex, interesting, an amalgam of many characteristics. They will, in the main, be busy raising families, working on the family farm, too busy in fact to create much in the way of records at all. The strategies discussed in Chapter 7 on writing about characters can help counter this aspect of writing family history.

The slippery world of words

Reading published family histories, I find many instances of inadequate English expression. I have found pages of jumbled text, or paragraphs that are too short or paragraphs that are incoherent, wordy and overlong. I read sentences that do not have verbs, and sentences that are far too long. I have found paragraphs that are disjointed and disconnected where the writer has not bothered to think about how one paragraph might link to the next.

A paragraph should have a clear theme—many unrelated or incoherent ideas in a sentence or a paragraph might suit a wordy academic, but it is not what your reader will thank you for in the family history.

As historians we are also artists, we are creating language that should have a rhythm, a style, a pleasant resonance to our eyes. At the same time your use of language should be grammatically correct. The grammatical rules or conventions you studied at school are likely to be long forgotten. However, it is relatively easy to check word usage and grammar in writing and editing books as well as in books on English usage.

As noted elsewhere, do not be too concerned about these issues when you are writing drafts. It is when you are rewriting and editing that you can weed out generalisations and poor word usage with a good dictionary and editing manual.

There are some excellent websites providing straightforward advice on sentence and paragraph construction so as to avoid the 'slippery world of words'. The Purdue University online advice on writing is aimed at students but is useful for the general writer. It can be accessed at <http://owl.english. purdue.edu/handouts>.

The University of Kansas provides a comprehensive list of writing tips, guides and useful advice at <http://www.writing. ku.edu/students/guides.shtml>.

Repeat, ~~repeat, repeat~~

In history writing it is easy to fall into the trap of repeating the obvious. We write such phrases as 'looking back to the past', 'past history', 'return back', 'follow after', 'early beginnings' or 'descend downwards'—and we rarely notice until an eagle-eyed reader or editor notes our mistake!

The same word can crop up in your writing almost as though a glitch has occurred in the word processor or your mind. It is not possible to always see this repetition until you begin to edit.

For example, you might use the word 'good' in one sentence, such as 'she was a good woman', then a few sentences later, write 'they had a good year', and then in the paragraph following, write 'their lives had brought them good fortune'. You may not notice the repetition without a concerted effort to examine your writing and edit out these anomalies.

A useful strategy is to have a dictionary and thesaurus open as you write, and consciously look for words that explain what you want to say in a more appropriate way.

Instead of saying 'she was a good woman' you might now write 'she was an interesting woman who read books from the local library and enjoyed a spirited conversation about local politics'.

It is easy to repeat ideas, events and descriptions about characters, or to repeat entire scenes from one part of your text in a later part. One way of overcoming such duplication is to put your manuscript away for a few weeks or a month. Then re-read and edit and re-read it again. Ask a friend or colleague to read the text, and edit out some of these repetitions and glitches for you.

A family history is made up of a complex array of facts, ideas, further research and assumptions. Writing it, refining it and making the task more manageable will take time.

Take your time working through the text. Enjoy it. Immerse yourself in your writing, and your family history will be the better for it.

Clichés, jargon and slang

Clichés are words or expressions that are in fashion for a while, but are overused and lose their impact. For example, 'deep and meaningful', 'actually', 'gross', 'everyday life', 'society', 'this day and age', 'old adage', or 'sadder but wiser'.

Although traditionalists suggest you stay away from slang, if it survives in the language, it can, if used appropriately, evoke periods of history well. Words like 'chook', 'whinger', 'bludger' and 'mob' are part of the Australian idiom and can be used, especially in dialogue, anecdote or conversational writing. If you do use slang or clichés intentionally or out of context, it is useful to place these in quotation marks or use italics as in 'bludger' or *bludger*.

Jargon adds little to our writing and is best avoided. Some of the worst examples in current usage include: ISP (Internet Service Provider), promo (sales promotion), esoteric (understood only by those with special knowledge), and polemic (a controversial argument).

If what you want to say is worth writing about, then try to say it clearly and concisely without resorting to clichés or jargon.

Abbreviations and shortened forms

Use as few abbreviations and acronyms as is possible. There are many acronyms and abbreviations cluttering text these days and readers soon tire of them, especially in a family history where they are reading their own stories, or at least, the stories of extended family.

Always spell out the abbreviation in full the first time you use it, with the shortened form in brackets if required; as in Australian Broadcasting Corporation (ABC). After the first mention, you can then use the abbreviation or the name in full.

Some common shortened forms are used without explanations, such as Mr, Dr, Jr, Sr, pm, am, and the symbols kg, mm (without a full stop). Abbreviations used in footnotes or text such as p., vol., or ed. are followed by a full stop. If you are in doubt when using an abbreviation or shortened form, check the AGPS *Style Manual: For authors, editors and printers*.

Unnecessary words

Underlying our use of overstatement, eulogising the family, and being too wordy with our writing, is the use of what Strunk and White refer to as 'too many unnecessary words'.[4]

Recent examples from family history include the much overused 'the fact that', a phrase often cited as an example of unnecessary words. The following examples are from Strunk and White:[5]

Needless Words	Use Instead
the question as to whether	whether
there is no doubt that	no doubt
used for fuel purposes	used for fuel
he is a man who	he
in a hasty manner	hastily
this is a subject that	this subject
owing to the fact that	since
in spite of the fact that	though
I was unaware of the fact that	I was unaware
the fact that	because

Non-discriminatory language

You have an obligation to that wider community of readers, researchers and family history groups to use non-discriminatory language in your writing. You will find an admirable chapter on non-discriminatory language in the AGPS *Style Manual: For authors, editors and printers*.

Discriminatory language can emerge when writing about race, ethnicity, gender, disability, age and sexuality. When quoting racist, sexist or other demeaning words from past eras or documents, you should note that this is a quote and reference accordingly.[6]

Verbatim quotes from a letter or primary document can present such problems for the writer. For example, these arise when you are writing about the conflict between white Australia and Aboriginal people. Using terms like 'marauding blacks', a term sometimes found in original documents and older texts, without an appropriate context is discriminatory. As a family historian, it is your task to be even-handed and critical when you encounter these terms and when you then write about the events connected to them.

I faced this problem when writing about my great grandmother. She operated a popular and well-known private maternity hospital in Kempsey from the early 1900s to the late 1930s. As far as I know, she did not confine any Aboriginal women. According to other sources, Aboriginal women gave birth on an isolated veranda in the local public hospital and were kept well away from white patients. This shameful practice continued until the 1960s.

How did I write about this? I wrote at the appropriate point that Mary Kirkpatrick did not confine Aboriginal women and the following paragraph I put in my conclusion:

I do not know of course what kinds of attitudes Nurse Kirk and her sons held about Aboriginal lives. I suspect they accepted the prevailing racism, they certainly benefited from such colonial divisions. My great grandmother and her sons were able to purchase land; hard won perhaps, but still a choice they could make. They could profit from it, secure their place on the coast.[7]

Being professional

Most of us have a story of an ancestor who was supposedly related to a royal line or who might have been a famous musician, politician, chieftain or rebel or related to one of these interesting characters. For most of us, it will be just that, a story embellished by time but not able to be validated through research.

Keep the story on file and include it, where appropriate, with the qualification that there is no verification of it to date. Writing about these myths and legends will add colour to your family history and ease your writing pathway.

Each story, legend or not, opens a window into other writing and new ways of seeing the family history. The following story from my father's maternal ancestry is a good example. The story of Robert Hobbs's life and times in the Windsor district would have been relatively uneventful if it had not been for his will; the contents of which were to linger in the family memory to suggest that there was some kind of Hobbs millions, a sum that was to climb in ensuing years to a figure of 3 million pounds. Douglas Bowd outlines the story in his book.[8] The story seems to have begun when, a copy of his will made shortly before he died in 1839, Robert Hobbs wrote that he 'claimed possession of freehold estate in London'. He wrote:

> *... left to John Hobbs my brother of Spitalfields in his will*
> *of 1814, I bequeath the said property share and share alike*

to Robert, Mary, Elizabeth, Harriet, Edward, Joseph,
Catherine, John and Sarah.

(He left 'one third to his wife and two thirds to his
children. Also, £3,500 in consols bearing interest at 3 per
cent, which . . .)

I consider has been deprived from me by fraud and
want of integrity on the part of one Caleb Wilson and
Company of Sydney.[9]

Over the one hundred years after Robert Hobbs's death,
reports on the Hobbs millions and his will appeared regularly
in the press. However, a grandson of Robert Hobbs, one W.
McKenzie, reported in 1926 at a family reunion that he had
been investigating the wrong Robert Hobbs and the 'mythical
millions faded like the morning mist'.[10]

In addition, as Bowd adds, the only 'lawfully begotten'
child was the last-born Sarah and only she would have had
a claim if this story had been true.[11] Unfortunately, for the
descendants of our Robert Hobbs, the mythical fortune
belonged elsewhere.

As a child, I heard these stories of the family connection
supposedly to a large inheritance. My sceptical mother would
say to me, 'They're all a bit mad you know!'. This was her
assessment of what she suspected was a family myth. It is too
good a story to leave out of the family history, however, and
I would include it, acknowledging the fact that it is only
a mythical fortune that no one in the family can expect to
find at all.

Brilliant characters, marvellous events

Writing with passion can sometimes lead to undue emphasis on the historical significance of an individual or family in the past. The following examples were written recently (I have changed details to retain anonymity for the writers):

> Dedicated tradesman, esteemed genial community and business leader, property owner, all-round sportsman, supporter of a range of charities and a number of sporting organisations, and devoted father of twelve. John Albert Smith was all that, and more.
>
> The story of this extraordinary pioneer begins at Athlone, County Roscommon, on the 6th January, 1833, where he was born, the second child of agricultural labourer James Smith (1800–1880) and his wife Margaret Brown (1803–1884).

Overstatement in this way is a common occurrence in our writing as we try to construct an interesting portrayal of characters and their journey in the past. Early drafts can be overblown and far from concise. You should try to eliminate this overwriting when you edit final drafts. Take note of the 'blazing sunsets' you find, and check carefully how well the adjectives and adverbs sit in the text—this will be a beginning for later editing of your manuscript.

Look at the nostalgia, sentiment and passion you feel for the family history as entry points for your writing. Draw on that passion and the memories of your older relatives to enliven the text.

At the same time, use the accepted rules and conventions of historical writing, and remain as objective as is possible through accurate and consistent referencing and sourcing. Evaluate and eliminate bias in research and writing by checking the authenticity and accuracy of research data through as many points of reference as you can.

However, in the end, how you write and what sort of family history you publish will be determined by emotional decisions you make about how you and your family connect to that past.

Use passion as a starting point for writing evocative stories and re-read, revise and edit as you learn more, become more confident, and develop a greater sense of the place of your family in that long past.

Example

The following excerpts are from *Poppy* by Drusilla Modjeska:

It's all very well for me to make grand statements comparing one generation with another, but there's a limit to what you can learn that way; there are too many complexities and qualifications. Generalizations (sic) are a weak form of argument. Perhaps I'm asking the wrong questions, battering at the painful episode of Poppy's breakdown when the answer I want is not to be found in the wound, but in the way in which it healed. Is it the fact of her recovery that makes Poppy interesting? She was not doomed, to madness or to history. There wouldn't have been a story to tell if she'd ended up as one of those women who are kept in the back room with shapeless skirts and blank eyes, an embarrassment to the family.[12]

Drusilla Modjeska's *Poppy* is not a biography but a mixture of 'fact and fiction, biography and novel'.[13] She used fictional names for family members so as not to embarrass them. Modjeska's explanation as to why she decided to write her mother's story in this way alerts the reader to the complexities of writing about 'truth' (in the past) and to the fact that this story is fictional. She writes:

To stick to the facts seemed to deny the fictional paradox of truthfulness, and the life that the book was demanding. On the other hand, to give up the facts, and the serious pleasures of history and biography, would have defeated the purpose with which I began.[14]

We could all take a lead from Modjeska's willingness to be honest about her approach to storytelling. As historians we need to 'keep it real', too.

EXERCISES

- Scan the daily newspapers for examples of clichés and jargon.
- Read Drusilla Modjeska's *Poppy* or Frank McCourt's *Angela's Ashes*—Note the sensory details these authors use in their writing.
- Take an imaginative walk through the place where you lived as a child. It may be a house where you lived, a beach from your youthful surfing days, or the place where your grandparents lived. It might be the place where your original ancestors lived.
- Walk through the rooms, imagine the doorways and where furniture was located. Imagine that you are walking near trees—Are they orange trees loaded with fruit, or an old apple gum with its tortured straggling limbs, or do you see Norfolk pine and smell the pungent tangy aroma as the pine needles are crushed by your feet? Do you hear the ticking of the grandfather clock, or the floors creaking? Is that your grandmother standing at the kitchen table, with flour up to her elbows as she kneads the dough in a heavy china bowl? Imagine yourself in many places and try to use all of the fives senses in your writing.
- Draw the spaces and the structures and make a note of where things happened, such as where the food was cooked and where people slept. To begin your sensory journey, write a paragraph or two describing the structures and spaces you find. Try to evoke the sensory detail of the place—the sounds, smells, tastes, touch and what you can see.

- Allow yourself time to rewrite and edit your own work. Check each word, phrase, sentence and paragraph carefully. Do you really need every adjective? Look for specific problems: long sentences, sentences without verbs, awkward or over-flowery phrasing, vague or too abstract wording, overstatement, stating the obvious, tautology, and unclear or woolly ideas.

The art of history

Writing family history is a balancing act between using the passion and nostalgia you feel for your family and using them wisely to write professional stories. The passion and nostalgia can also aid the writing process; it can help inspire the ideas, the words and the compassion to find a language to write stories with affection and critique.

Writing history is an art as well as a science and its language should have rhythm and tenor. Read your writing aloud. Listen to how it sounds as well as how it reads on the page.

Chapter ten ↻

HISTORICAL CONTEXT IS WHAT?

Too many things to think about and you cannot get started? Historical context is what? Relax and read about how to stop thinking and start writing...

Too many things to think about

Too much conflicting and confusing advice is overwhelming for beginning writers. Sometimes it is downright unhelpful.

You are told to keep your words pithy, your sentences short, and adjectives few! And, as well, you are told to have a good 'sense of the past'. How can you do all this in the straightforward family history you are writing?

It is a wonder that anyone would put pen to paper so worried are we about all of the advice we read! Although my advice, or any other advice on writing, is useful, do not let it overwhelm you. It should not be a barrier to getting started, to telling your story and getting it into print.

Historical context adds a broader frame of reference to your family story. But you should not worry too much about it until you have sorted out how to start writing and have something on the page.

Everyone has a different approach to getting started with their writing. Most of us will use a computer for our writing and editing. Many people now use a computer for all of their writing including first drafts.

When I am writing new stories, or constructing a story from new material, I use pen and paper for the first draft. I spread my resources—books, documents, press reports, certificates, transcripts, letters and articles—around me as I sit at my desk. I need to work out visually how they relate to one another and sort through them as I write. It is only when I have a first draft completed in old-fashioned hand-writing that I turn to the computer. Each of us will have a different strategy for writing drafts and moving on to editing and incorporating previously written material.

The big picture

Incorporating historical context is about connecting your approach to writing history to other historical views on history. It is not a difficult nor a demanding task—adding in the 'big picture' is, after all, the linking work that all good history writing should do.

Each story is unique, that is true, but each story is familiar territory too. Family history is universal history. Birth, death, marriage, work, love, hope, joy, anguish—these are common to all families, even in the long past.

As historians of our family, it is our job to link our stories, as much as it is possible, to the drama of neighbourhoods, to the hopes and dreams of local communities, and to the ebb and flow of national themes, as we relate the events of the everyday battles of our own families throughout history.

Writers draw inspiration from many sources; memory, everyday experience, reading, work, film and television. The literature we read—novels, biographies, historical and travel books, and the news section of newspapers—all provide creative stimulation for our writing.

Some years ago, as the only family historian at a history seminar, I argued that professional historians could hardly expect family historians to link into their work when it remained so obtuse and inaccessible. With the rise of cultural studies and the demise of traditional history at universities, this remains little changed.

It would make more sense, of course, if we were told that historical context is nothing more than comparing your family history against other historical writing. That is, historical context is about comparing your family history against the bigger picture of national and international events.

Family historians are not writing academic theses, and there is no need to make your story into a dreary academic dissertation. It is wise, however, to be alert to the range of histories already published.

There is a plethora of Australian and overseas history titles available in public libraries, and these offer background information on every aspect of the family, from women's history, the history of childhood, stories of convicts and immigrants, to local history, Indigenous history, economic history, and the history of public institutions such as schools, churches and community organisations.

Do not be intimidated by academic language in these books. On the contrary see the books as good friends that can add to your skills as a writer. They can certainly ease the history writing process.

Do not re-invent the wheels of history by assuming you are the first person to discover the 'facts' of Australian history. Your story is unique, but there will be a book somewhere that has beaten you to the ideas, the events and the broader contexts of family and other histories.

Read around your ideas, theme or stories, and you will garner many different ways of supporting your story, enhancing it, and easing the writing process. Although writing family history is your personal journey, you remain part of the larger enterprise of history.

Writing family history is a mixture of:

- Writing from documents
- Seeking the truth
- Searching for identity
- Good English expression
- Correct grammar and punctuation
- Correct spelling
- Telling stories
- Describing characters
- Interpretation and imagination
- Writing from the heart
- Writing with passion
- Writing within the rules and conventions
- Avoiding bias, prejudice and stating the obvious
- Seeking to write about the past
- Not everything in the past
- Journeys
- Writing about a past we can never know exactly
- The use of evidence, ideas and research
- Not made up.

Interpretation, assumption and imagination

There are basic historical events that are well known. The dates and general outline of major political, economic and social events, such as world wars, need little introduction. Also widely known are the reign of monarchs, depression eras, economic booms, the introduction of social or political reform legislation, and other national or international happenings of world history.

When writing about any of these events, it is not necessary to elaborate except when certain dates or events might be in dispute. You do not have to rewrite history—but simply use and incorporate those parts of it relevant to your family story.

We interpret and assume all kinds of things about people, relationships and news events as we take part in our community, as we shop and as we interact with our family. We use interpretation every day to sort through the daily minutiae of our lives. It is a skill we already have; and it should be an easy matter to transfer this to the writing of our family stories.

For family historians the fundamental interpretive task centres on primary documents such as birth, death and marriage certificates. We search for names, dates, events, occupations, origins and work histories. We search through the records of land, buildings, education and immigration for dates, names, land purchase, schooling and voyage details. We record these dates meticulously. And it is from these lists, these family statistics about our past, that we then construct our family stories. Moving from these facts to writing family history requires the use of this interpretive process.

Interpretation is that practical task where you pore over your documents and sources, extracting facts, ideas and themes to begin to write. It is also using those ideas and the themes you draw from your documents for your writing.

With interpretation you can create a compelling story that you imagine happened because it fits with the facts, legends, stories, hopes, dreams and characters of your family. At the same time you need to keep your imagination within the bounds of historical accuracy, authenticity and validity. The assumptions or conclusions you make ,as you interpret your documents have to be credible, believable and historically accurate.

My imagination got the better of me!

You cannot claim to have descended from royalty if it is not true. You cannot make your characters any more or less able than they really were. But, you can imagine, interpret and assume—from your evidence, from your family stories.

Through interpretation of available facts and examination of the wider historical context, you should be able to draw together the many threads and themes in your family history. And with some imagination and judicious assumption, you can add colour and flair to the family history story.

Assuming that certain things happened in your family, however, is different to claiming or inferring inappropriately.

It is important when writing any kind of history to distinguish between those things that are 'true' and those that are not.

You can assume or infer around an event that does happen; such as a birth, a death, a marriage, a work incident, or a convict or immigration experience. But you cannot make up stories about your family and publish them as family history.

All generations of historians, including family historians, have a fresh perspective to bring to their writing. They may have the use of new documents released perhaps for the first time. Or they may challenge accepted orthodoxy with fresh ideas drawn from social or political movements like feminism, economic rationalism or post-modernism.

Working class history will be different to histories of the ruling classes. Women's history will provide a domestic, perhaps family-oriented view of history that we had not thought about before. The history of childhood can add challenging views to ideas on the past.

The histories of minority groups, Indigenous Australians, the histories of newly arrived migrants or the histories of people with disabilities will also bring ideas and inspiration to add to your view of history.

History is not fixed. It is a constantly changing, ever-challenging debate. So use your imagination as a starting point for writing, but keep within the bounds of historical accuracy and check what you plan to write against the wide range of research and writing

already published. History can be interpreted but it cannot be made up.

Using your interpretive skills

When I was writing the life story of my great grandmother, I knew she nursed her dying daughter for two weeks just before Christmas 1882 because it said so on the death certificate. I knew it must have been cold because it was winter in Belfast. But that is all I knew. It was enough, however, to write the following story and say something about her character and the impact that event had on her life:

> Mary Kirkpatrick had sat beside the bed for two weeks bathing her daughter Janet's tiny feverish body in warm water and feeding her sips of warm broth and milk.
> She bathed the secretions from her eyes and nose and gently rubbed the child's hot forehead with a cold compress.
> Mary knew about illness and death as she had seen her own friend's children slip away like this. She had read about childhood illnesses and medicine as she had an interest in the field. She knew too much to think her daughter would survive but not enough to save her.[1]

For other sections of my family history, I had even less factual information. However, as I continued to write and tried to fill in the gaps, I was able to suggest or infer that certain things were more likely to have happened than others. I could say that my great grandmother responded in certain ways because of this issue or that. In the last chapter of my book, I wrote the following to further alert the reader to my interpretation and use of imagination in the writing of the family history:

> As I move toward the end of Nurse Kirk's story I realise I have so little information about this woman; there are too few documents, only a smattering of archival papers, no family letters, only fragmentary memories. I can trace her movements year by year only because she advertised her work and her hospitals, often and in changing detail, in the local press. But still I do not know enough about her despite my more than twenty years of research, despite my efforts to chart the family relationships, my concern to try and understand that past. The windows into her life remain opaque, shadowy... Much of what I have written about Nurse Kirk's life is about probability; she probably did this, thought that, was driven by some things, not others. There is no certainty here; just a faint beating memory of this lone mother battling, working, scheming, making her mark along the coast.[2]

For most of us, such probability and uncertainty will be all we can hope for as some, indeed most, of the 'facts' of our family stories are lost forever.

Conveying a sense of the past

There are some aspects of history writing that make it different to other writing. One is that rather elusive idea that we need to convey a sense of the past. If we were writing a thesis, we might call this historiography or perhaps shaping the content or telling the stories. As you write, it is all and everything you do to be authentic, credible, interesting, readable, trustworthy and as historically accurate as is possible.

One of the ways in which writers fail to convey that sense of the past occurs when they fall into the trap of over-simplification and overgeneralisation. They do not interpret words and expressions well for the historical period they are writing about.

Additionally, where there is personal bias, poor reporting, distortion of evidence, or insufficient evidence for your interpretation, there will be a poor sense of history in the writing.

Writers new to history can fall into the traps of inadequate or poor citation, are less than convincing in their use of source material, and pay too little attention to critical editing of their drafts. But do not be discouraged. Even the most experienced historian will make the mistake of oversimplifying or over-generalising from time to time. The trick for the writer of history is to be aware, to try to eliminate, and to revise, rewrite and edit your work so as to make it as professional as possible.

Breaking down the task

The belief that you have to write it all and write it all now is widespread. No writing task, however, is so big or so complicated that you cannot break it down into more manageable pieces.

For family historians, breaking down the writing task into smaller pieces makes a lot of sense. You can write short biographies, a story of one generation or a family, or short pieces on places, people or events, and file them away. Each of these can provide a starting point for later writing.

As the chronicler of the family past, you have to sort and draw together a disparate and diverse, not to mention large, body of factual material. Your research base eventually becomes unwieldy, indeed overwhelming, in its scope, range and size. It is made up of a great many computer as well as paper files, and no doubt these continue to amass. It is true, as already noted, that genealogical software is useful for sorting names and dates; but it cannot establish themes, ideas or stories from the data, and nor can it write the family history for you.

At some point you have to sit down and write a family story that makes sense of all the research you have done.

Your writing and your interpretation of the data will be easier and more professional if you look more closely at your use of words,

syntax, sentence structure, paragraph placement, and the general tenor of the language on the page. A little attention to this as you write will pay dividends for the final shape of the book.

Incorporating previous history

A relevant question I am often asked is how to incorporate previous history into the writing of the family history. I am asked how the family historian can use previously published or unpublished family history in their work, and also how to incorporate the larger stories from local, national and international published histories.

In other words, this question is about the 'nuts and bolts' of placing your family history within a broader historical context. What should you be thinking about, and what issues are relevant, as you draw on and incorporate other sources?

You incorporate the information you select as relevant to your family history from these sources in the same way and within the same historical rules which you follow for all sourcing and referencing. These rules and conventions include the following:

- **Plagiarism**—Is taking sections of other people's writing (no matter what it is) and passing it off as your own. This includes diagrams, maps, charts, photographs, illustrations, full quotes and material taken from websites. You must always acknowledge other people's work by using footnotes or referencing.

- **Permission**—Is needed if you want to use a direct quote from your source material and it is considered to be a substantial portion of the work. What constitutes a substantial portion varies depending on what is being copied and from which kind of text. For example, a few lines from a song or a poem may be considered substantial and therefore require written permission from the copyright holder.

- **Copyright**—Begins at the time of creation and normally ends 70 years after the creator's death. If the work is never published, the copyright continues indefinitely. Copyright protects the way an idea, information or factual data is expressed; that is, the way in which it is written in text, such as in a story, non-fiction book, article, poem, treatise, play, song, novel, newspaper article, set of statistics or a table, catalogue or directory. The actual idea or information cannot be protected. Therefore, if you paraphrase the text or idea in the same way in which the previous author does, you will need to acknowledge that source.

- **Moral rights**—Basically, among other things, recognises that an author has the right to expect that you name them in respect of their work and you do it correctly in your writing.

- **Photographs**—Are subject to new rules of copyright since the introduction of the Australian and United States Free

Trade Agreement (AUSFTA) on 1 January 2005. Unless the photograph is taken for private or domestic reasons, the copyright is owned by the photographer.

Copyrights on photographs now last until 70 years from the end of the year the photographer died. If the photographer is unknown, copyright lasts from 70 years from when it is published. However, all photographs taken before 1 January 1955 are now out of copyright, as the 70 year legislation was only introduced in 2005.

The Information Sheet, *Duration of copyright*, published by the Australian Copyright Council (G23) on its website, has detailed advice on the operation and expiration dates of copyright for photographs and other material pre- and post- the AUSFTA. See <http://www.copyright.org.au>.

• **Defamation and libel**—Laws vary from state to state but there are principles which can be applied to determine whether persons are being defamed. It is no defence to claim that you did not intend to defame the person or that a mistake was made. However, the laws of libel are unpredictable.

There is no guarantee of success or of failure in the courts. Normally what has to be proved is 'damage to reputation'; this is much more easily done if you have a few direct quotes or facts but much harder if, in the case of a novel or academic treatise, the text is more abstract, dense and wordy. It is not possible to defame the dead, but it is possible to defame the relatives of the dead.

Stating the obvious

Your reader does not have to be told that Brisbane is in Queensland or that Sydney is in New South Wales. They will, however, need to be told where that small village in the highlands of Scotland is, or the location of an obscure town or station in remote Australia. But telling your reader obvious facts about your family, a country or well-known historical events is unnecessary.

Example

Childhood experiences and your relationships with significant adults are rarely expressed well. In the following example, 'The Music Teacher and the Milkman' by Dawn Montgomery, the author tells the reader that this is a family story with the comment '. . . into our family lore'. Her story is set within the context of how a child's perceptions about parents are often universal, and that we can be surprised, as adults, with the knowledge of how passionate, and how human, our parents really are.

> My mother and my father met quite by accident really. She was waiting to cross the road one day when along came George in his shiny black automobile and ran her down. He picked her up and dusted her down and asked her out to dinner. About a year later they were married, and the

195

way they met passed into our family lore. Almost sixty years later, after Mum had had two strokes, a broken leg and a fractured hip, Dad and I were following her up our front stairs one day. Dad was shaking his head and looked all 'choked up'. I asked what was wrong.

'Look at her legs, how scrawny they have become. She used to have such great legs.'

'Good heavens, Dad I didn't know you were a leg man!' My parents had always seemed peculiarly asexual to me, as I guess most parents appear to their children.

'Oh, yes,' he said. 'That's one of the reasons I married her. That's what caused the accident.'[3]

Recognising and incorporating aspects of race, gender, ethnicity, age and class, as well as country, county and place, in your writing of the family history will bring your stories to life and give them greater authenticity. Nowhere is this more striking and more necessary than in writing about our European ancestor's initial contact with Indigenous people. The following excerpt from Ann McGrath's story about settler's perceptions of Aboriginal workers in nineteenth century Northern Territory illustrates the need for historical context:

One manager had induced a white man to enter his employ by offering him the pick of the best 'black velvet', informing him and other employees that there were plenty more down in the camp if they wanted them, and that he would go down and procure them for a small fee. Black women were viewed as a side benefit of working on remote cattle stations. In one instance a white pumper on an isolated outcamp had sent a message to the manager demanding either a new pumper or a young 'gin'; he was sent two girls.

EXERCISES

- Temper your use of imagination in family history with relevant facts. Read background history for the time periods you are writing about, as well as for the different regions and countries.

- A general history of the place, time period and context for your family history is a good place to start your reading. You can select more specific reading as you become more knowledgeable about it.

- On your next visit to a public library, browse the shelves for published family history, biographies, autobiographies, memoirs and life stories. Take note of stories that catch your interest. Look at recent published history, biography and memoir in your local bookshop, too.

- Compile a sample family history outline for the first part of your family story. Try to add as many possible themes, ideas, sources and further leads for research as you can think of. This is the beginning. Although it may seem rough, this outline will help you begin the construction of your roadmap or plan for writing.

Getting on with it

Use the accepted rules and conventions of historical writing, and try to remain as objective as is possible through accurate and consistent referencing and sourcing of your work. Eliminate bias in your research and writing by checking the authenticity and accuracy of your research data through as many points of reference as is possible. But you also need to get on with it. You need to start writing, now!

Stop thinking and start writing. Most of the advice on writing can be applied to the words once you get them onto the page. But you have to get the words down first. So write quickly and edit later. Write from your imagination and check this against your facts. Interpret, make judicious assumptions and stay true to your story

Chapter eleven ❧

SHARE THE WRITING JOURNEY

S haring the journey is a key strategy for easier writing. Sharing words, ideas, plans and reservations about writing engenders confidence, creativity and motivation.

A shared activity

Sharing our family stories, our data, our sources and our interesting research with other family historians increases our ability to find out more about the family history. Sharing research questions, information on libraries and archives, useful internet sites, new sources and ideas with our friends and colleagues in family history is the first step to becoming more confident and knowledgeable about our research. Attend the monthly meetings of your local family history group and you will soon find out how beneficial sharing can be.

Local family history organisations have, as their basic premise, the principle that sharing, one to one, and within the group, is important. I have attended many of these meetings and have marvelled at the wealth of information-sharing that takes place. And such sharing will work for writing family history, too.

The writing journey

It is a truism to say that we are all different. Each of us will write differently about the family. We certainly have similar stories to tell (of flood, fire, drought, family conflict and family relationships), but our experiences, our approach to the writing and our perceptions of family events will differ.

Your memories of childhood, how you remember parents, the relationships you had and have with siblings, your recollections of grandparents, your experience of growing up, of marriage, of your own parenting, of work, leisure and friendships—all of these will have a bearing on your writing.

You will be delighted, surprised and enthralled when you listen to and share the writing journey of others, and discover how different and how diverse your writing and their writing can be.

To have the advantage of reading another piece of writing, in all its versatility and difference, and to know that it is no better and no worse than any other, but just different, is a salutary lesson.

It is vital to celebrate that difference and draw on the writing lessons that can be taken from sharing stories with others. You will gain confidence as well.

When you read your writing to others, or listen to others read their writing, you can be astonished, enchanted, captivated and supported by this simple act. Yes, it is true that some writing will be assessed as more literary or as more readable or as somehow 'better', but that assessment is a subjective one that has no place in a shared writing session. In my experience, if members of a writing group write honestly and with passion, each piece of writing will be as 'good' as any other.

Sharing your writing is a key strategy for improving writing skills, for instilling confidence, and for recognising that there are many, many different ways of presenting family stories to readers. The starting point for sharing is to join like-minded writers who are also on a writing journey. Joining a writing group, learning creative writing or attending workshops will provide you with inspiration for easier and better writing.

Joining a writing group

A writing group is NOT a workshop or a formal course. You will not be taught how to write and nor will there be a teacher whose duty or purpose it is to present lessons on writing.

Rather, a family history writing group is an informal 'coming together' of writers to listen to others, to share ideas on research and writing, and to provide support and information of all kinds about the writing and publishing process.

A key aim of a writing group is to learn through interaction with other writers. These writers may have a very different writing style to your own, but they can open your eyes and your creative energy to new ways of telling, thinking and writing about the family.

I have been a member of many writing groups over the years—creative writing groups, informal writing groups, fiction writing groups and non-fiction writing groups. I have benefited from sharing writing ideas, from the support of other writers, and the critique they have offered on my writing and my ideas. I have benefited from listening to writers read their work, and express their fears, their joy and the frustrations they feel about their writing. I have been transported into unusual and creative worlds of writing and reflecting on new ideas, often at an exhilarating pace.

I am always on the lookout for seminars, workshops, writing discussions, radio broadcasts, festivals, exhibitions— anything that is focused on my general interest in writing.

Writing is a solitary, isolated and very personal task. You can benefit, however, from the inspiration and support of others to continue your writing.

> Just meeting with a writing friend over coffee is sometimes enough to break down barriers to easier and more professional writing.

Starting a family history writing group

There may not be a writing group within your family history society. If this is the case you can join with like-minded individuals and start a writing group of your own: it is not difficult.

Approach your local family history society and ask them to incorporate a writing interest group into the list of interest groups organised by them. Your local family history society may be able to organise a meeting space and advertise your meeting times in their journal. Ask to speak at the monthly meetings of the society and invite members to be part of the group.

However, it is not necessary for you to be part of any local organisation in order to enjoy the benefits of sharing. A writing group can be two or three people meeting over a coffee at home or a local cafe. You might be able to meet at the local library. Make enquiries as to what access you can have to local meeting rooms in a library or other local community building.

Writing group do's and don'ts

There is no right way to organise your meetings. Some beginning writers prefer a structured meeting. In that case ask each member to nominate a topic for 'homework' and map out a program; for example, fifteen minutes of discussion, then each member can read their story written about the topic, allow time for further discussion, and have a break for a chat.

For those who do not like a structured meeting format, it might be enough to simply arrive at the meeting and allow a free flow of conversation, to listen to each other's stories and to discuss various writing issues that are affecting individual members.

It is not necessary for all members to have similar writing interests. You do not have to like someone in order to learn from them.

Following are some important points to consider to ensure your family history writing group begins well, and is open to change and challenge.

Limited membership

Try to keep member numbers down to ten people or less. Any more than this and it soon becomes difficult to allocate time for individuals to read their work or share ideas.

Meeting time

Two-hour meetings seem to work well. Allow time for housekeeping, catch-up news and general chatting.

Meeting program

At the beginning of each year, put together a program of meetings with dates, the name/s of topics, possible facilitator/s for each meeting and timetables.

Rotate leadership

Rotating the leadership of the group meetings reinforces the principles of sharing that underly the group. It is a lot to ask one person to take on the responsibility of booking meeting venues, planning and preparing programs, and facilitating and supporting members at all times.

A writing group is about sharing, and one person should not be expected to somehow meet the needs of everyone in the group. Rotating leadership will also engender confidence in new members, and ensure a supportive and professional environment is developed.

Reading and sharing

Reading your work is a key strategy to improve your writing skills. But it is time-consuming. I have found that members rarely stay within word limits unless strict ground rules are established at the outset. The word limit for reading aloud should be no more than 500 words.

Most beginning writers find it difficult to stay within a strict word limit. Impress upon members that this is simply a 'summary' or 'excerpt' from a longer piece of writing. They can always write more but the reading is a special event and has to be brief to fit the rules and timetable of the group.

If the word limit is not enforced and some members continue to read more than they should, others will not have an opportunity to read. If a 500-word limit is not possible, limit membership to five or six.

Reading and feedback

Few of us are experienced in providing feedback to other writers. 'That was good' or 'I liked that' are common, unhelpful responses. Or worse, the feedback session becomes a general chat about how each member's family history is 'just like that'.

Try to encourage members to say why they like the piece (was it the humour, the pathos, the surprise ending) or how they think the piece could be expanded for the family history.

Inclusiveness and tolerance

A family history writing group can be a meeting ground for very different writers. Some members are more focused on self-development, writing memoir or autobiography, while others want to stay specifically focused on traditional family history.

Although there is a common interest in writing family history among the members, there will need to be a willingness to accept, and see the strength of, difference and diversity in the group. Talk this through with members and ensure every member has input into determining where and how the group will proceed.

The group is not working

Sometimes you can outgrow a group and it is time to move on. Or, from the outset, you might feel this is not the group for you; perhaps it may be too structured or not structured enough for your liking.

It is best to be open about your feelings and share your concerns. You can then decide whether you should stay or move to a more appropriate writing group for your developing writing needs.

Example

The following notes were made after a writing meeting on a topic titled 'Music and Your Family History'. The notes illustrate how different but how individually compelling the stories of the participants were.

Our stories began with Yvonne who told us how the enchantment of music was threaded through her life. She has sweet musical memories of her mother's soprano voice as well as of her own performances in musicals including Reveller's Revue. Yvonne attended dance classes when young, thought for while she might become another Shirley Temple, but when reality clicked in she fell in love with classical ballet and in her late teens took up ballroom dancing (at the Trocadero). She was given a piano for her tenth birthday and began music lessons. Yvonne sat her pianoforte examinations at The London College of Music, Sydney Branch, which were held in a building behind Palings, and spent hours around the piano with her family. These days Yvonne's dancing is a little more sedate but the musical memories and the music still remain to engender movement and rhythm at this gentler but still evocative pace.

Tanya grew up with music in the home, with her mother winning many radio 'Guess that tune' competitions, but at our meeting thought she did not have a music story to tell. She thought at first she might not be able to write about being a musician, but when she told her sister about it, she said, 'You gave me my first guitar! And so began Tanya's story. Tanya's story was about the bonds within her family and how music helped to forge those bonds. She said there was a heritage of the love of music going back to Northumberland, England, where her maternal family owned an inn where they welcomed and shared playing and singing together. Tanya forgot to tell us until the end of the group session that her love of music showed in her love of dance. She had taught folk dancing to children, danced in a Coca-Cola commercial that won an international award and had been involved in many musical productions.

Hazel began by saying she was tone deaf, but she and we do not now think this is true. She could remember her mother singing when she was quite young, and remembered the songs. Her mother and father went to all the dances, where children would fall asleep under tables, in washing baskets. These were elaborate dances where fancy dress was common, her mother winning many prizes for her dress. This was in the 1930s... Hazel remembered her aunt had a wind-up gramophone and played Paul Robson and Gracie Fields, which she loved. Hazel said she was taught music at high school, but it was not a good experience. It was when she learnt ballroom dancing at the age of fifteen that her liking for movement and rhythm, and her love of music really flowered. Ballroom dancing became her obsession and we might call Hazel's story, 'Give me five minutes more!'—one of the tunes she remembers from those times. Hazel loves country and western, and soft, dreamy music, and her story was also one about how music wound its way through the family and continues to weave its spell.

Jan's story of the double bass and her battle with taxis and buses as a young woman going to and fro to rehearsals gave us all food for thought and just a little laughter! Jan studied in London and played at Oxford and Cambridge universities with the Chelsea Opera Group, conducted by the now famous Sir Colin Davis. As she said, one day Cambridge, the next the world (and those battles with public transport). 'Has she got a ticket for that thing?' should be the title of Jan's story—from a question she was asked by a passenger before she scurried off a box carriage one day. In Australia, Jan toured with Opera and the Ballet Company Orchestra, and was at the opening of the Opera House. Her grandmother was a talented pianist and Rudolph Meyer, who played for King Christian VIII of Denmark for twenty years in the mid-1840s, is an ancestor. Jan's story was amazing—a life of music on the stage, a great deal of dedication and a host of memories...a fantastic journey.

Barbara's story began with the comment that she learnt to type to music, and we can still hear that ping as she got to the end of the line on the old manual typewriter! Barbara said there was always music in her family; her earliest memory is her father playing his ukulele—there were many war songs—and she and her brother would march around the kitchen...she was probably about three years of age. As children, they made up songs, went to sleep to jazz, she learnt to tap dance, and she loved dancing and concerts. Barbara had many memories of stage presentations doing the highland fling, and she learnt piano briefly. Her mother is a pianist and at 87 has restarted her playing... She remembers family members playing the spoons, the comb and paper, the gum leaf and the saw. Her sister would sing and her mother sang around the house. Her father and grandfather played the drums. Her father played at school socials and in several orchestras including Bright Lites. Music was a creative spark in Barbara's family and its memory continues to generate the emotions, the feelings and the links to bring past and present together.

Lybbie began by saying that, 'Music is what feelings sound like?' Her mother's father, George Gale, was Welsh and singing was then a way of life. A song conveyed everything; girls sang and played piano. The weekends, for her mother, were spent at the local picture theatre watching old silent black and white films, and the interval music was provided by the family. Lybbie's mother was taken out of school quite young but her mother insisted she learn piano and do examinations in pianoforte. After her mother's marriage music was not allowed as Lybbie's father did not like music in the house, and sadly she was not allowed to learn. Her mother did not restart piano until she moved to Alstonville as a widow. She now plays daily for at least one hour.

Lois, in her early years, was engaged to Neville who played viola in the Sydney Symphony Orchestra. It was her first love, her great romantic journey as a young and beautiful woman (I know you didn't say this, Lois, but we know it was so ...), but alas her aunt talked her out of her romantic liaison with the viola player (who, by the way, sat in the same orchestral pit as Jan, and that link generated some great discussion). Lois's mother was a pianist and a singer, and Lois has a memory of her mother singing softly to the baby, humming to the baby. Then the teenage years kicked in, and Lois went off to the big bands and flashing lights of dancing and fun. And then she discovered the world of great composers and a different music. Music enriches her life and has been integral to her life journey, Lois said. She had an album of music and dance programs of events she had gone to over the years to show us ... Lois also sang in musical theatre, and she said she hoped that her 242-word essay was music to Noeline's ears!

Jill's story reminds us again of mothers, music, family and memory. Jill's mother made Jill her first long frock when she was twelve; Jill was going to a special dance and was concerned her young brothers might not behave. She danced that night with her father—a wonderful experience, as he was a great dancer. And the Edwards brothers, so handsome, asked her to dance. A special dance, a special time ... Jill said she was involved in the lighter side of music and has just written out all of the old popular songs for a family reunion. She enjoys all music and has sung in choirs. Most of her life has been lived in small towns, which unfortunately did not provide the same opportunity for music and dance and theatre. But she is always ready to dance. The fellas were gorgeous then, she said, and she enjoyed the dances very much. She loves listening to any music but especially loves Hymns of Praise on Sunday TV. Once again, music, rhythm and movement are so much a part of a journey through life ...

When we first gave out the topic of music (Lybbie's idea), most of us thought, Music? I do not think I could write a thing about that! But it turned out to be one of our best sessions. There was romance, drama, conflict, betrayal. Well, not betrayal—I made that bit up! But music in family history certainly stirred many emotions and generated fantastic stories for the group. Each story was different and the telling unique to the person. But each was absorbing nonetheless.

EXERCISES FOR SHARED WRITING

Listening to others read provides a scope for self-improvement, comparison and the building of self-confidence. The family history writing groups I have facilitated preferred a structured writing program with exercises or topics set for each meeting. There are many books available on writing where you can find exercises, tips and ideas for sharing in a writing group.

Look at Dianne Bates's *The New Writer's Survival Guide*; Julia Cameron's *The Artist's Way: A Course in Discovering and Recovering Your Creative Self*; and Paulette Gee's *How To Stop Stalling & Start Writing The Story of Your Life*. Also useful are Kate Grenville's *The Writing Book* and *Writing From Start to Finish: A six-step guide*; Patti Miller's *Writing Your Life: A journey of discovery*; and E. Murphy's *You Can Write: A Do-it-Yourself Manual*.

See also my book *The Family History Writing Book* and this title, *Writing Family History Made Very Easy*, for ideas, questions, topics and guidelines on starting a family history writing group and developing topics for it. Search internet websites on writing and writing family history for further ideas.

The following is a brief list of exercises you can use in writing groups.

- Select a wedding photograph, and write a story about it.
- Write a story about a letter or a diary.
- Choose a family artefact (a piece of jewellery, household item or crockery) and write a story about it.
- How is music reflected in or was part of your family? Write a story about it. Do you can have photographs, recordings, dance cards or posters to illustrate the story?
- Write a story about a Christmas that was memorable in your own life, perhaps when you were a child, or were at work. Was it a sad Christmas? Poignant? Funny? Happy? Frustrating?
- Describe a place, a room or a landscape or some other kind of environment from your family history. What's the time of day, the weather, are you in the city or the country, are you inside or outside, is it hot or cold, is it a pleasant place or not, what can be heard, seen or smelled? Were you told about this place by a parent or grandparent?
- Write a letter to your grandmother *from you now*. It can be about your memories of her, or 'what if I had known you' (if she died before you got to know her well), or it can be questions and comments on what her life was like in that historical time.

- Your group might like to use a meeting to discuss the more technical aspects of writing. Editing is a thorny issue for all of us, both when we do it ourselves (often badly) and when others do it for us (and we become upset and angry as we misconstrue as unnecessary criticism what is simply useful and critical feedback). Other issues of concern include referencing, copyright, privacy, permissions, incorporating previous history, indexing, poor English expression and how to fix it, point of view, characterisation, defamation and self-publishing.

- Try free writing exercises. Ask each member to include a surprise topic (about a character, an event, a family conflict, a school incident or a personal story) and give members 5–10 minutes to write one or two paragraphs. Members can then read their writing in turn and provide feedback.

Chapter twelve ᐁ

CHOOSING YOUR FORMAT

What format will you choose for your family history? Have you studied all the options?

Why are you writing this family history?

There is no doubt we write so that future generations will know something of the family history. For most of us, however, writing is a solitary activity and our own children and grandchildren are rarely as interested in that long past as we are. We hope our writing of the family history will at least provide a record for when they do show an interest later.

Our writing of the family history will be there for grandchildren to read when they are older and perhaps more interested to learn about the childhood, life and times of ancestors. In their old age, our grandchildren and great grandchildren can be charmed by the detail that is of little concern to them now while they are young.

Which format you choose to write your family history in will depend very much on *why* you are writing this family history and *who* you are writing for. Only you can determine that format. As the writer, you make the choices and you establish the parameters of the family history.

There is little doubt that most of us will write, hoping that future generations will have a record of the past. At the same time, we can be motivated to write and publish in a particular format simply because we become more knowledgeable as we do further research. I have been asked the question, Which format should I choose?, many times. The answer to this question and the format you choose will depend very much on your collected data, your family stories, and the characters and events specific to your family history.

A search for identity

Writing family history can be, and often is, a search for identity. In Australia few Anglo-Australians know their family origins unless they are a middle-class family with a well-established pedigree.

The rest of us, especially if our ancestors arrived in the first decades of the nineteenth century, know little of the history of our great grandparents and nothing of those first arrivals until we do the research.

For family historians this initial search, and finding the names and stories of first arrivals, is a thrilling event. A need to 'belong', or a fascination with a 'family myth' or a desire to trace female ancestors can drive our writing task as well.

Finding names and stories that are meaningful and connected to our family adds depth, meaning and interest to our lives. Writing and publishing the family history provides a tangible and provable link to that past for future generations.

A *special character*

As we research and write, a special character can emerge and we want to write their story so that it will survive.

As Chapter 7 on writing about characters reveals, family history is about people; and writing about special characters is a useful entry point to beginning writing and a suitable format for the story itself.

Most family historians find that at least one character emerges and captures the imagination much more than the rest. Perhaps it is the story of a mother or father, a grandparent or great grandparent that takes us on the writing journey and more firmly toward writing the family history.

A *family reunion or anniversary*

Publishing your family history to coincide with a significant occasion, such as a parent's or grandparent's 80th or 90th birthday, can provide motivation for writing. As can a family reunion where extended family are potential buyers as well as appreciative readers.

Personal experience

Grief, loss, divorce, adoption, an abusive childhood, abandonment, a family tragedy, a major accident or retirement can be emotional triggers for writing family history.

The emotional impact of a physical trauma or of a major illness can be devastating, but can also be a time for re-evaluation of who we are and where we are going in life. The loss of a parent is an event that many of us are surprised to find engenders a desire to know more about the past. We find ourselves reflecting on the life experiences of parents, and of their parents, and our journey as a researcher, writer and family historian then begins.

Many reasons

In the end, your reasons for writing and then deciding to publish in a particular format will be based on a combination of any or all of the above.

If you are writing your family history to coincide with a parent's birthday celebration, a family anniversary or a family reunion, the format of your book may tend toward a more traditional structure. If you prefer to record the story of a favourite character, a biographical format might appeal.

The writing of a family history after the loss of a parent

or grandparent is a more personal writing journey and may be written and published as a memoir. The search for identity can lead the family historian into diverse approaches including a local, regional or occupational focus.

If your extended family are involved in the decision-making about final publication and contribute toward research costs, you should hold discussions with them early in the research and writing so that everyone is clear about what the final format will be.

The following list of writing formats range from basic compilations through to ficition and memoir. Do not limit your choice. Writing family history can be done in many genres. Take your time and choose the format best suited to your writing and your family.

The pedigree

Traditionally, family history is written as a list of names together with some biographical material and with genealogical charts either in the text or in an appendix.

In general constructing a pedigree or chart is a useful strategy as a background to, and aid for, writing the family history. This basic list of names and dates provides an accurate and consistent set of data to more easily gauge the scope and range of your material. It also enables you to see more clearly the various relationships and significant links between individuals and families (especially if you are working with a long line of descent from centuries before the nineteenth).

However, if this is all you do, then you will limit the value of your family history as a piece of history. The length, number and complexity of the charts generally make them almost unintelligible to all but the most persistent reader. In addition, the pedigree approach tends to minimise women's names on the family tree.

Books such as Angus Baxter's *Tracing Your Origins* and Gerald Hamilton-Edwards's *In Search of Ancestry* contain the beginning rules associated with developing a pedigree format for a published family history. Nancy Gray's *Compiling Your Family History* remains one of the best guides for Australian writers of family history. Dom Meadley's *Writing a Family History* has useful information on constructing and including charts. Meadley also directs the family historian towards Patrick Malgrave Moore's *How to Record Your Family Tree* to find detailed rules and principles to construct genealogical charts. The websites of local, national and international genealogical societies can also help. Search the following websites for additional information on constructing a pedigree:

- Misbach Enterprises,
  <http://www.misbach.org/pdfcharts/>
- Genealogy Research,
  <http://www.cmail.cz/mraz1/genealogy_research.html>
- The Federation of Family History Societies,
  <http://www.genfair.com/shop/pages/fed/page01.html>

- Family Tree Magazine,
  <http://www.familytreemagazine.com/articles/feb03/soft
  ware.html>
- The US Genweb Project,
  <http://www.usgenweb.org/research/starting.shtml>
- Family History & Genealogy,
  <http://www.bestgenealogyresearch.info/>
- Cyndi's List of Genealogy Sites on the Internet,
  <http://www.cyndislist.com/>

One generation at a time

Writing one generation at a time can be a useful format for your book. By focusing on one generation, your publication becomes the first volume or first edition of the family history. You might choose to write a second book or edition later, covering subsequent generations or another member of the family.

The one-generation-at-a-time format can be structured as follows:

- The first generation can be the first family to be written about.
- Only those ancestors possessing the family name or who were members of the first arriving family would be included, thus confining both the familial and the historical time period under study.

- The book can be confined to the local geographical region as far as is possible, although this may be difficult for some family history where frequent internal migration is a feature of early history.
- The family history is limited in its time span (for example, from arrival in 1789 to the death of the first arrivals in 1842).

By setting these familial, geographical and date parameters, you can immediately construct a manageable and logical framework for the writing task.

A compilation of documents

Since I wrote about compiling a set of documents into a family history in 1993 in the *Family History Writing Book*, an interest in scrapbooking and handmade books has emerged. Scrapbooking, in particular, offers a format that can be easily modified and used to construct a family history.

Simple compilation

This is a simple compilation of the more important certificates, photographs, newspaper clippings and other items. A simple compliation can be completed as follows:

- Purchase an archival quality folder with clear envelopes.

- Place copies of the documents, with relevant notations and headings, in a logical chronological order in the envelopes. Additional envelopes can be purchased as the compilation grows.
- Write the name of the family, name of compiler and the date on the front of the folder. Make some comment on the first page of the compilation about any other additional information that you hold and where other researchers might access it.
- Write a forward, preface or introductory chapter briefly outlining your research journey and/or goals and some information about the format of the compilation.
- List your sources in a bibliography and add a contents page.
- Deposit a copy in a local genealogical library, with the Society of Australian Genealogists, or in your State Library or local or regional library. Keep the original for yourself and family in an archive box.

Simple compilation with notes

This format is similar to scrapbooking and can be modified to suit that approach:

- Purchase a heavy ledger-type book (archival quality).
- Compile handwritten and typed notes on each generation of the family. Use the guidelines for compilation as described by Nancy Gray's *Compiling Your Family History*.

- Add copies of photographs and other relevant documents where appropriate.
- Write the name of the family, name of compiler and the date on the front of the ledger (or take it to a printer to have the title and other information inscribed).
- Make some comment on the first page of the compilation about any other additional information that you hold and where other researchers might access it.
- List your sources in a bibliography and add a contents page.
- Photocopies can be made of the finished result and the photocopies bound by a printer.
- Deposit a copy in the local genealogical library, with the Society of Australian Genealogists, or in your State Library or local or regional library. Keep the original for yourself and family in an archive box.

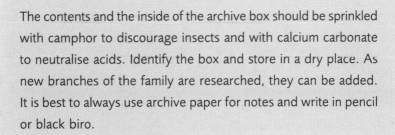

The contents and the inside of the archive box should be sprinkled with camphor to discourage insects and with calcium carbonate to neutralise acids. Identify the box and store in a dry place. As new branches of the family are researched, they can be added. It is best to always use archive paper for notes and write in pencil or black biro.

Copies of your compilation can be sold or given to other family members. If family members have helped with gathering information and providing original material, such as letters, photographs and other family memorabilia, a copy of the compilation can make an ideal gift to show your appreciation.

The National Archives of Australia has a free information leaflet 'Caring for your family archives' on its website <http://www.naa.gov.au/recordkeeping/rkpubs/advices/advice10. html>. It contains advice on packaging, storage, handling and use, and common problems and questions for family historians preserving collected material at home.

Chronology

To write chronologically is to start at the beginning and work systematically through the various stages, generations, events, names, dates and families. This constructs a family history that is based on the exact sequence of how the time periods and events have occurred.

Using a chronology to work out the framework of the historical project remains a useful strategy for organising family history.

If you peruse the shelves of any library, you will find historical publications where there will be a series of chapters, each of which is marked by the time period it covers; for example, 1788–1820, 1821–1840, 1841–1860, 1861–1880 or 1881–1900. Under the designated time period, the writer will include all of the known historical and family events that occurred.

The basic rationale of traditional genealogy, where the line of descent is traced through father and sons, is recorded easily in this chronological way. With the shift to a broader definition of family history, and less emphasis on the male line and a greater focus on the female members of the family and the children, a chronological framework remains a useful format for many published family histories, but it may need to be combined with some biographical, memoir or other thematic formats.

Themes or topics

The use of a thematic approach is possibly the second most popular organising principle used by historians. In family history, themes have usually been centred on commonly occurring historical aspects such as convict origins, occupations or immigration.

Other themes that could be of interest for the family historian are those associated with childhood, education, the lives of women, the changing family, religion, depression years, war service, war and home, leisure activities and sport.

Most family historians will choose to write their family history within a format that includes some aspect of time periods and within these the important topics or themes will be located. This is a perfectly sensible way to arrange the text and as noted earlier, you will likely choose to include other genres of writing, such as biography and autobiography, as part of the writing plan as well.

Local or regional history

Framing the family history within a particular local region provides the writer with an organising principle to set limits of geography but with considerable scope in the range of topics to be covered.

If an individual family does reside in a house for a long historical period, the building and its history become important for Australian history, or at least for the local region in which it is located.

In addition, researching a house and land can be particularly rewarding, providing a rich source of social history, by documenting the changing trends in household activity, land and building use. Within this format, the family can then be located as the human agents who interact with and provide the momentum for change in society, culture and the environment.

Occupational history

I have read excellent family histories where the occupational history provides a strong framework for the writing and the publishing of the work.

Using occupation or professional experiences as a framework for the family history provides a convenient entry point into the very heart of the family—work determines class, status, where one will live, the kinds of friends and leisure one chooses, and the original reason for emigrating to Australia.

Therefore, if done well, this format can produce a family

history that addresses a range of important social and economic questions while it documents the family history.

Mary Durack's *Kings in Grass Castles* is an occupational family saga documenting a pioneering cattle family in the Kimberley region. There are many examples of published books focusing on teachers, religious figures, doctors, nurses and business leaders in the genre of occupational family history.

Institutional history

I am thinking here, in particular, of a school, a club, an organisation or a government agency. Many individuals in the past were significant members of such institutions and writing a family history incorporates a major part of the history of the institution as well.

Some well-known examples include B. Bolton, *Booth's Drum: The Salvation Army in Australia*; D.G. Bowd, *Lucy Osborn c. 1836–1891: Founder of the Nightingale System of Nursing at Sydney Hospital*; and J.H. Donohue, *The Catholics of New South Wales 1788–1820 and their families*.

Immigration

After biography, generation by generation, and chronology, immigration is the most popular means of writing about ancestors. Family historians learn very quickly that they must obtain the death certificates of their first ancestors as this enables them to calculate the time of arrival in Australia.

A death certificate will sometimes give the place of origin as well. Of course, why your ancestors decided to immigrate in the first place will most likely depend very much on the actual political, economic and social context of the country of origin.

When looking at the histories of these places, you will find that for the period of time during which your ancestor left for Australia there may be specific and common reasons for immigration; some involved large scale immigration to Australia due to poverty or because of particular political conflict. Personal reasons can include the death of a wife, husband or child, the loss of employment, a downturn in the local economy, or family conflict.

In general there are two main kinds of immigration: the individuals who chose to come to Australia of their own free will; and those who did not, including convicts and the military personnel who were in charge of them. When you do succeed in finding reasons for immigration, you may find that the same family has been part of a longer history of migration, for example, from Scotland to Ireland (because of religious persecution) and then to Australia.

The arrival and settlement of your ancestors in Australia provides a focal point for your story as families begin their work and establish themselves in particular local regions or in newly settled rural areas.

Convicts and criminality

For those ancestors who arrived as convicts, you might like to document your family history around that initial transportation and the ways in which the succeeding generations coped in Australia.

Convict and criminal records provide considerable detail on physical appearance, and sometimes personal characteristics and behaviour, making for writing that is more evocative. There is also a diverse and rich field of research and publication already on convicts and criminality, making your task as a family historian all that much easier.

Economic and political history

The economic stresses that families faced in their place of origin and in Australia have produced particularly poignant and passionate accounts of family life.

Bushranging, transportation of political prisoners, the Eureka Stockade and other political protests in early Australia, participation in and support of the labour movement, strikes at the workplace, religious persecutions, the suffragists, and many other political activities framed the lives of our ancestors in the past.

What part did your ancestors play in these economic and political upheavals? Did such events shape the economic future of the families? You can gauge some of the economic and political parameters of family life from facts related to property ownership, where individuals lived, who they married, what they thought about their relationship to their original homeland, and the work they did, and how these factors changed over time and across generations.

Biography

Writing the biography of a favourite character can take your writing away from the more traditional format. I used this approach to write the story of my great grandmother. Although I utilised the research and writing approaches of traditional genealogy, such as chronology, maps and charts, names, dates, photographs and the chronicling of family relationships, I did so within a biographical framework.

Writing about one person does not preclude writing about other characters in your family history. You will find that to write accurately you will need to examine the lives of wives, husbands, sisters, brothers, parents, grandparents, friends, business colleagues and indeed enemies. A biographical approach might also provide a local focus if your character and the family lived for most of their lives in one place.

Traditional genealogy charts generations from the long past to the present time, normally through biographical sketches of important characters in the family history. This approach continues to be used today, with the presentation of lists of original ancestors (with biographical material as far as is known) listed down to the latest born child.

Unfortunately, for some family history, a biographical approach can also lapse into what we might call a 'mini-cv' approach to family history. This appears with the inclusion of names of living persons, normally towards the end of the book, as writers try to summarise source material provided by extended family members.

We are presented with short summaries detailing where young Johnnie, Sarah, Lily, Ada or Rebecca went to pre-school, how much they like animals and snowboarding, how many times they have been to New Zealand, and their dates of birth.

This is not history. Nor is it family history.

For example, for young children the biography or mini-cv I regularly read is something along the following lines:

Elle Ann Brown was born in Bundaberg on 8 January 1994 to Joy Smith and Peter Brown. Elle attends pre-school at Bundaberg State School. Elle is a bright, open child, enjoys performing and chats freely. She likes to do beading and craft.

Or, a mini-cv can also be used as for a young adult, as in the following entry:

Jane Smith wants to build a career around children. She loves children and would like to work with them. Her primary school education was at Bowen State School and Kelvin Grove. Jane is in Grade 11. Away from school, Jane takes singing lessons and is involved in sport and theatre.

These short pieces of information read simply as achievement lists, or resumes of hopes for the future. For the older person, this approach leads to the inclusion of outright promotional text:

The year 2001 produced a complete change for Susie Brown. She gave up a lifetime career of working at a wide range of jobs to become a full-time mum, caring for her husband and three children. Before 2001, Susie had worked as a receptionist, cook, shop assistant, cleaner, and in an office. By the time Susie was ready for school the family was living in Sydney so she went to a state primary school from Grade 1 to 6. Grades 11 and 12 were completed at Sydney Girls High School. Susie worked for a year at Smith & Sons, a firm in Waverley, after she completed high school. Her next position was with a spare parts shop in South Sydney...

If you choose to include living relatives in your family history publication, and have permission to do so, it would be far more relevant to bring a particular line of family research up to date and write something like the following:

John Smith and Mary Ann Brown were married in 1985 at St James, Melbourne, and moved to Bendigo late the same year. John works as an accountant for Centrelink and Mary Ann teaches kindergarten classes at the Bendigo State School. They have two children, James who is 8 and Eliza aged 4.

It is difficult to find a balance between writing stories about our current family (whom we love and care about) and the family history. Perhaps a good rule for writing about the present is to use the advice that 'less is best' — and keep your descriptions of them professional and straightforward.

Autobiography

An autobiography has only one author and is written by the person herself or himself. Writing in an autobiographical mode is often a mixture of literary (the use of dialogue or fictional approaches) and historical techniques (detailed research into family, local and other histories).

A fine Australian example is Sally Morgan's *My Place*, a search for origins and roots (as in family history), which raises complex issues of racism and poverty at the same time as it tells a human and lively story.

With autobiography, there can be a tendency to reduce the life to the mundane or the prosaic and tell a long list of irrelevant facts. Autobiography, to be compelling and creative, relies to some extent on the writer's willingness to probe into difficult areas of the life—few of us have the writing skills of Sally Morgan and even fewer are willing to be as truthful because the resultant exposure of family secrets, tragedy, hurt or grief is too painful for all concerned.

Memoir

An autobiography is the story of a life, the term implying that the writer will somehow capture all the elements of that life. A memoir, on the other hand, does not replicate a whole life.

One of the fundamental aspects of a memoir is the selection of a theme or themes that link events, people and stories to a unified and overarching frame. It needn't tell a complete story of a life, but rather select aspects of it. Most people write only one autobiography; you can, however, write many memoirs.

Memoir, as distinct from family history or autobiography, is not based on meticulous, systematic research. It may have research attached to it, but is more often a recollection of the past. Memoir is less about history and more about perceptions of the author on their life, and on other people's lives and events. Recent successful memoir writing includes Kim

Mahood's *Craft for a Dry Lake*, Inga Clendinnen's *Tiger's Eye: A memoir*, and Drusilla Modjeska's *Poppy*.

Unlike autobiography, memoir writing is not necessarily based on fact. Writing memoir is a more personal approach, and requires close attention to ethics and issues of truth and examination of questions around 'whose story is being told'. We can also descend into sentimentality or fall into the trap of writing as though our lives and our experiences are somehow more desperate, more painful, more illuminating or more unhappy than most! Worse, if they are not, we are tempted to make them up so that we can be all of those things and more.

Writing a memoir, as in autobiography and biography, and in writing history, is about real people. Those people deserve respect and recognition. You cannot give them a character or personality, ideas, activities or attributes that they really did not have. If you do not have the evidence to back up your writing of the memoir or autobiography, then you cannot invent it to add spice to your story. If you do, you are writing fiction and the reader deserves to be told that fiction is the format rather than history.

Fiction

Although writing family history is a task based on research, and has at its centre the ultimate goal of producing a record of exact family connections and relationships, it is also inevitable that much of what constitutes the family history has now been lost. We can retrieve many of the relevant dates and names, but almost always we lack information about people, how they coped in the past, what they thought of the social and political changes of their time, and their daily experiences of schooling, home and work.

Sometimes we have photographs to show us how particular individuals looked when they were married or when they were children, but we have little idea of the clothes they wore every day, the household items they used or the manner in which they travelled, or how these changed over time.

Cherry Cordner's *A Mavis Singing: The Story of An Australian Family* is a family history presented through a fictional genre. She used conventional research techniques, and drew on a wide range of archival sources to develop the narrative and the geographical and economic parameters of the actual family history. The presentation of her story is through a fictionalised version of the family story told through the persona of her mother Mavis. The 'I' of the story is Cherry Cordner but the story is about Mavis, her sisters, her mother and her grandmother. The family tree chart is situated on a page at the beginning of the book so that readers can refer to it when needed.

A Mavis Singing is a lively and well-written family tale. The first paragraph sets the scene and tells the reader immediately that this family story is being told through two sets of memories; that of the daughter and the mother. Cherry

Cordner's book is fiction and we are never in any doubt about that.

Creative non-fiction

Creative non-fiction is a form of writing where the approach is fictional but with the writing said to be largely based on fact.

Well-known examples are Alice Sebold, *Lucky*; Truman Capote, *In Cold Blood*; Bruce Chatwin, *In Patagonia*; Frank McCourt, *Angela's Ashes*; Hunter S. Thompson, *Hell's Angels*; Kim Mahood, *Craft for a Dry Lake*; and Inga Clendinnen, *Tiger's Eye*. Norma Khouri's *Forbidden Love*, James Frey's *A Million Little Pieces*, and Helen Demidenko's *The Hand that Signed the Paper* are also written in this genre but were exposed as largely fictional although promoted as 'truth' by the authors and publishers.

There is nothing wrong in choosing creative non-fiction so long as the reader is aware the lines between fiction and fact have been blurred. It is sometimes difficult to find that line as publishers and writers seek to have their turn at producing a best-seller.

Creative non-fiction, like memoir or fiction, can be used for writing family history. The reader should be told at the outset, however, that fictional devices are in use and that the story being told is

not true, or is true only in part. Like memoir, creative non-fiction requires scrupulous honesty between writer and reader.

Some fictional techniques are not acceptable in history writing: for example, the creating of a fictional character and presenting them as real is simply a nonsense in history. It is also not acceptable to present fictional events as true activities in the family history. You cannot invent a whole section of your life or your family's life, nor can you make up a 'better' outcome or ending. You cannot write that a house burned down, or a drowning occurred, or that a journey took place, if it is not true.

As a family historian you have a contract with your reader to be as truthful as is possible. While speculation has its place, if you cross the line from fact to fiction without telling your reader, they will be skeptical about your presentation of all of the family history.

Letters, cookbooks, photograph albums

A collection of family letters together with other documents and relevant stories can provide a format for your book. Cookbooks and recipes passed down in the family can also frame the family history. Women's lives, in particular, resonate through food, cooking, sharing recipes and traditional family events and this format can highlight and make more visible their lives.

New media

New media technology has led to new formats, such as books composed of photographs with limited text, or an oral history recorded on CD or DVD. Some family histories are published on a website.

In most instances these new media formats are additional to a published book or part thereof.

Example

The following example of creative non-fiction in family history comes from *A Mavis Singing* by Cherry Cordner.

We had a castle in the family. Doesn't everyone? It had always been there, in the terrain of memory, together with the uncle who lived in a tree, the relatives who spent their lives at Fannie Bay Goal, and, the cousin who blew out his brains on a railway station and remained forever in a gaslit pool of blood... It was my mother who re-created this world for me. She was surrounded by a whole galaxy of star performers involved in great firecracker moments.[1]

EXERCISES

- Talk to your family and/or other family history colleagues about the format best suited to your family history publication. Talk to other family historians about their plans and approaches.
- Read widely. Browse the shelves of libraries and bookshops for recently published memoir, biography, autobiography, family history (including fictional approaches), creative non-fiction, personal stories and other family history.
- Study the books that appeal most to you. Look at how the authors use language, explain their approach and structure their text.
- Can't get started? Record yourself reading your stories aloud, transcribe it then use this as a basis for beginning a plan, developing new ideas and starting the task of writing the family history.

Chapter thirteen ✑

PUBLISHING YOUR FAMILY HISTORY

Congratulations! You have completed writing the family history. Read on for practical advice on how to turn it into a published book.

Printing and publishing

Printers are not publishers. They do not design, edit, proofread, market or distribute your book.

A publisher, on the other hand, accepts the completed manuscript and will edit, design the book and cover, organise typesetting, printing, binding, publicity, sales, marketing and distribution, and pay you a royalty from the sales.

The number, range and quality of small desktop publishers and printers has increased dramatically over the last ten years, with more widespread and proficient use of computers, scanners, digital cameras and colour printers of high quality.

There is no doubt that you will find a form of publishing to suit your family history story. Following are some of the commonly used forms of publishing for family history.

Self-publishing

Most family history will be self-published. Self-publishing means you organise and pay for the production of your family history title—from editing, typesetting and design, to printing and distribution.

Peruse your phone directory under Printers General to find small publishing firms and printers in your area—there will be many to choose from. Following is a brief list to begin your search:

- *Adelaide Proformat* Ph: (08) 8371 4465, 5 Windana Mews, Glandore, SA, 5037. <http://www.jaunay.com/publishing.html>
- *Fast Books* Ph: (02) 9692 0166, 16 Darghan Street, Glebe, NSW, 2038. <http://www.fastbooks.com.au>
- *Griffin Press* Ph: (02) 9412 6111, Fax: (02) 9884 8940, Level 13, 67 Albert Avenue, Chatswood, NSW, 2067. <http://www.griffinpress.com.au>
- *Hippo Books* Ph: (02) 9313 7811, Fax: (02) 9313 7954, 18 Primrose Avenue, Rosebery, NSW, 2018. <http://www.centatime.com.au>

- *Longmedia* Ph: (02) 9362 8441, 68 Oxford Street, Woollahra, NSW, 2025. <http://www.longmedia.com.au/lm_publish_now.html>
- *Seaview Press* Ph: (08) 8235 1553, PO Box 234, Henley Beach, SA, 5022. <http://www.seaview.com.au>
- *Southwood Press* Ph: (02) 9550 5100, 82 Chapel Street, Marrickville, NSW. <http://www.southwoodpress.com.au>

Vanity publishing

Vanity publishers agree to publish your work for a fee, often a substantial fee. They make no comment on, nor do they provide advice about, the quality of the writing.

Subsidised publishing

With subsidised publishing, the author pays the entire cost. However, the publisher will accept only those manuscripts they believe are of sufficient quality and meet reasonable commercial publishing standards.

Sometimes used to produce institutional or organisational histories, subsidised publishing might be an option when sales are not large but the publishing company believes the work is of sufficient importance and of a suitable quality to include in its imprint.

Using genealogical software

Genealogical software programs store the innumerable collected names and dates from our research. In addition, recent versions of these programs incorporate features similar to publishing programs like Microsoft Publisher. See the appendix for further notes on genealogical software and their functions useful for book production and self-publishing.

Other software

Most family historians use a word-processing program to write and prepare for publication. Some individuals move on to a program like Publisher or the more expensive industry standards Pagemaker, InDesign or QuarkXpress.

Euan Mitchell, in his book *Self-Publishing Made Simple,* advises the self-publisher to stay with Microsoft Word or a similar word-processing program, rather than using software that may be incompatible with selected printers or publishers.

The most prudent strategy is to ask your chosen printer or publisher how they would prefer the manuscript to be delivered. Most will say they want a hard copy and an electronic copy of your work, normally in Word or as a Portable Document Format (PDF) file.

Once in a PDF file, your document is fixed and cannot be altered. This function facilitates the printing and publishing process, and protects your submitted text from undue alteration or corruption (as often happens in large Word files when you change from one computer or program to another). Few of us have the full version of Adobe Acrobat, however, to do the conversion to PDF file.

Writing your manuscript in Word, or Word Perfect, is the simplest, safest and most sensible format for self-publishing. Unless you are an expert, leave the conversion to PDF, if required, to your chosen printer or publisher. They should be able to convert your files to their requirements professionally and easily.

Costing

Costs are normally shared in the researching, writing and publishing of family history. If you are sharing costs then discuss all aspects of this at the outset with your fellow authors or compilers. Make decisions about costing or other aspects of the book design at the beginning of your research and writing, not at the end.

The more colour, the more photographs, the more pages, the glossier and better quality the paper, the better quality cover—all will add to the cost. It is cheaper if you do the formatting yourself and provide a disc or hard copy to your printer or publisher.

As an example, a book published recently had 166 pages, A5 page size, and ten black and white photographs scanned from prints. A desktop publishing firm did the formatting and copy editing, and designed a colour cover. The initial print run was for 100 books. The unit cost of the book was $10 plus $7 for set-up costs. When reprinted, the cost of the book was $10 per unit. This is a fairly typical costing example.

According to some experts, a self-publisher should charge five or six times the total cost of producing the book—this will absorb distribution costs, and any discounts you provide (e.g. to bookshops and societies). Charging with this formula should give you back your initial outlay by the time you sell half of the books. On that formula, however, the cheapest price for the above example would be $50! Hardly an attractive proposition for our small family market.

Let us be frank here! This is family history you are publishing. It is not the literary event of the year! Just breaking even would be acceptable and a loss may well be inevitable.

A recommended retail price (RRP) of $20 or $22.50 for the above example returned the initial outlay and made a small profit. Most of us would be satisfied with such a result.

With digital printing, the unit cost will not vary no matter how small or large your print run. Therefore, start with a small print run and simply reprint as required. Do not make the mistake of thinking a larger print run (that has a cheaper unit cost with an offset printer) will be cost effective.

A good rule of thumb is to print a small number to test your market and then reprint with the proceeds of your sales as you

receive fresh orders. You might print 100 copies or as few as 50. Check with your printer/publisher for minimum numbers. Too many first-time self-publishers have made the mistake of printing 500 or 1000 copies of their book only to have them languish in the spare room unsold.

Professional editing or not?

Most family historians will try to refine their prose as they write. It is not easy, however, to be a critical editor of your own writing. You read and re-read poor sentence structure, your wordy paragraphs, repetitious prose and spelling mistakes, and miss most of them.

It is important, however, to become as critical as you can about your own writing. Whether you employ an editor or a proofreader will depend on your finances.

Paying someone to edit your work is useful but is no guarantee that the work will be mistake-free. However, a good proofreader can eliminate inept punctuation, poor grammar and repetitious prose.

Sharing your writing with a family history colleague can provide support and useful editing advice. Read each other's work. Discuss problems and provide constructive feedback to each other.

There are useful books on editing, including B. Kaplan's

Editing Made Easy and B. Ross-Larson's *Edit Yourself: A manual for everyone who works with words*, that offer sound advice to first-time writers and self-publishers of family history.

Book design

When you take your hard copy or disk to the printer or publisher, you will have the option of doing your own formatting and book design, or paying someone else to do it for you.

Formatting and book design can be done on a home computer but it takes expertise of a high order to produce a professional result.

Small desktop publishers have a range of prices incorporating some formatting and book design, and it is up to you to determine how much you can afford or if you can do it yourself.

The following website is the homepage of book and graphic designers in New South Wales http://www.galleyclubsydney. org.au/about/>.

Page size

Traditionally family history has been published in A4 size (21 cm x 29.7 cm) and this remains true today. The standard book size for most paperback publications is A5 (14.8 cm x 21 cm).

Midway between A4 and A5, is B5 (17.6 cm x 25 cm) and this can be chosen as a compromise. Another larger format, also used for non fiction or academic books, especially where there are many pages of illustrations, charts or other images, is C5 (22.9 cm x 16.2 cm).

Both A4 and B5 are regularly chosen in family history as these page sizes provide plenty of space for displaying photographs, charts and maps; A4 is also easy to self-publish cheaply. Keep in mind that paper quality, size and cost will vary with each printer and their advice will be crucial in your final decisions.

White space

Experts suggest that amateur publishers do not make enough use of white space. The first-time self-publisher may try to fill every space on the page with writing or illustrations, thinking perhaps that this is the way in which good publications are made. Wrong! The opposite is the way to go! White space is a way to rest the eye of your readers and can direct them to a feature or heading.

Imagine how much harder text would be to read if there was no white space? You use white space when you double-space writing and when you place double or treble spacing between lists of names or references. White space usually surrounds a heading, which is in larger type than the text, and is used around subheadings to denote importance as well as ease of legibility.

Attempting to save money by squeezing in more text and leaving small margins will send readers away. White space is important in page design. The reader will thank you for it.

If you examine good-quality magazines and journals, you will find that white space is used frequently in the general layout of a page, to highlight a drawing and as a setting for a photograph. On the other hand, take a look at the next batch of pamphlets dropped into your letterbox and note how crowded text mars the production of local or amateur productions. Liberal and judicious use of white space affords a professional finish because it is a practice that helps the reader to enjoy what they are reading.

Binding

Following are the common forms of binding used in book publishing:

- *Stapling, saddle stitching, comb or coil binding*—These economical alternatives are normally used for reports, manuals, cookbooks or other booklets with 70–80 pages or less. One disadvantage of stapling, saddle stitching, or comb or coil binding is that there is no place for the author's name and title on the spine. Librarians dislike these binding alternatives, as they are difficult to stand on the library shelves. These bindings are useful, however, for small print runs and for family historians who wish to do a trial layout and book design before final publication.

- *Thermal Binding*—Another cheap alternative with stapled pages and a heat-fixed plastic strip to cover the spine.
- *Perfect Binding*—This is the most common method and employs hot-glued pages inserted into a cover.
- *Burst Binding*—Similar to perfect binding, with nicks cut into the folds to keep glue dispersed; normally used for larger books.
- *Section Sewn (hard and softcover)*—The most expensive alternative and can add up to between $5 and $10 per book, especially with small runs.

Parts of a book

Deciding on an appropriate structure for your family history title is a crucial part of the researching, planning and writing process. Most non-fiction titles, including family history, follow a standard format, regardless of their page size or number. Look at the many existing publications to guide you.

The normal sequence for the main parts of a book is:
- half-title page
- title page

- publication details (on the reverse of the title page); included here also are the ISBN numbers and copyright notation
- foreword
- contents page
- list of illustrations (plates, photographs, figures, diagrams, tables, charts, maps)
- preface
- introduction
- main text (usually divided into chapters)
- appendices (includes family tree charts)
- bibliography (and/or references)
- glossary
- index

There is nothing worse than a haphazard littering of photographs and illustrations throughout the family history without any reference made to them. Where you place photographs, illustrations, maps and drawings in your published family history is important. Your reader will appreciate and understand them better if these are placed in text near to where there is a reference to them. For example, place the photograph of Great Uncle George on the same page as the story about him. A map explaining a local village or region should be located on the same page as your writing about these places. Also, be selective in your choice of photographs and other illustrations. Rather than including every photograph collected try to assess what each one will bring to the text and choose the one that is most relevant. Also, ensure that you have interesting captions and the names of individuals in the photographs listed clearly.

Present the documents used to gather information about the family either within the text (if appropriate) or attached as an appendix. Some documents are interesting enough or of such intrinsic value that you will want to reproduce them and place them in the family story. For example, a letter about a family illness or accident could be explanatory in the text in its own right, or a reference in a ship's register could provide a list of new arrivals at an important turning point in the family's history.

If you have an interesting will, such as where the deceased has included all of the family squabbles and their prejudices about the family, why not include it in full in the text? Other interesting documents emerge from school records, such as school reports or punishment records, providing amusing and sometimes extraordinary tales; again, these can be placed strategically in your text.

Do's and don'ts of layout and design

Be as sparing as possible with unnecessary formatting if you do your own layout and design. Euan Mitchell in his book *Self-Publishing Made Simple* has useful advice on text design and layout.[1] Here are some important points to consider.

Typeface

Do not use more than two typefaces in your text. Stay away from capitals in headings as lower case is said to be easier to read than upper case. Serif type (type with wiggles) is more commonly used as it is easier to read. For example, Times New Roman is a standard and 11 pt a customary size. For ease of reading keep text a reasonable size—never less than 9 pt. Sans serif type is useful for special purposes (say in a box) but not in a large body of text, while coloured text is much harder on the eyes.

Underlining is not normally used for emphasis in the text. Use capitals, italics or bold instead. Some underlining may be useful for charts when there are similar names or a need to separate generations.

Justify text or not?

Published books normally use justified text. However, if you are preparing a manuscript for a publisher, check first for their specifications before completing your formatting choices.

Margins

For ease of reading, do not set your inside margin too close to the spine, and set the inside margin a few extra millimetres (more than you think it should be in the finished book) to allow for the binding.

Start each chapter on a new page

The reader will not be pleased to find a chapter beginning halfway down the page!

Covers and spine

Bright colours are said to be best: the best-sellers in recent times are cited as lime green, electric purple, bright red or pink, or light colours. The worst colours to use are black, navy blue, olive green and dark brown.

This advice on colour for a cover is aimed at books that are destined for bookstores where busy shoppers browse and buy what catches their eyes. This will not normally be the case for family history, as most will be sold to and through family and not in bookstores.

The vogue in cover design changes and currently favours a matte finish. If you look at recently published books, the cover picture fills the front page and wraps around to the back cover.

Making the cover design too busy is the biggest blunder that family historians make. A perusal of covers on recently published family history reveals there is too much writing (long titles and sub-titles), a picture on a cluttered and poorly chosen background, and poor choice of text and colours.

Choose a picture that is appropriate to your story but also look at its design features. A picture or a photograph that has too much detail, or a map or chart with too many points of interest, will not work as well as a simple portrait or a striking building.

To finish your overall design, the back cover can include a short biography on the author/s and a 50-word description of the family history.

Most of us are not expert at book or cover design. We have a tendency to include too much text and try to squash in too many concepts and ideas. Your printer or publisher can help with cover design or refer you to a design expert. The cost may well be repaid with a more professional and pleasing result.

Photographs, illustrations, maps and charts

Charts, maps, photographs and other illustrative material will have to be provided in hard copy and on a disk or in electronic form so that the printer or publisher can insert them at the appropriate place in the book. You should ask your printer or publisher in what format they want photographs, illustrations, maps and charts delivered. Most commonly, they will ask for prints for the reproduction of black and white images and slides or transparencies for colour photographs (although good results can be had from colour prints if that is all you can provide).

Unless you have specific expertise, you will get a better

result if the printer or publisher scans images for you with more up-to-date and powerful computer technology.

It is more appropriate to use copies rather than the original photographs in your family history (if production is done at home). Original photographs are valuable historical documents and every care should be taken not to lose or damage them through inappropriate use of pastes or sticky papers. File them away in acid-free paper in an archive box. If you do decide to publish through a desktop publisher or printer, you can have suitable copies of the photographs made after you have discussed requirements with the publishing or printing experts.

To prepare your photographs, illustrations, maps and charts for delivery to the printer or publisher, you should:

- Make a photocopy of each, and place both the photocopy and the photograph in a plastic sleeve.
- Make a note in the manuscript where each photograph, illustration, map or chart is to be inserted; check with your printer or publisher how this should be done to their specifications.
- Write the caption on the photocopy, as well as the page number where the photograph is to be inserted, and the size you want it to be (quarter of a page, half a page).
- Clip everything together and deliver.

Choosing titles and alliterating ancestors

It is not new to find historians, and other writers, using alliteration as an aid to their construction of titles and headings for their works. Think of titles such as *Museums in Motion*; *The Triumph of Time*; *Finding our Fathers*; *Day of My Delight*; *Sons of the Suitcase*; *Mary of Maranoa*; *Punishment and Profit*; *Reluctant Revolutionaries*; *A Galaxy of Governesses*; *The Basis of the Bargain*; *Angela's Ashes*; *The Sewing Girls of Sydney*; and *Judge & Jury*.

Alliteration is a useful way of constructing a title for a book. Most publishers and authors consider a title in this form as a reasonable selling point for the work. Alliterated titles are catchy; they are picked up by the media and stand out on the bookshelf. In addition, juxtaposing opposing words and ideas (as in *Reluctant Revolutionary* or *Reform or Repression*) can be an aid to the writer and the reader, encapsulating neatly in a short phrase what the work is about.

Family historians, however, have turned alliteration into an art form. Titles such as *Peninsula Pioneers*; *From Skye to Sydney*; *From County Clare to Cootamundra*; *From Portsmouth to Portland*; *From London to Lismore*; or *From Glasgow to Griffith* abound in published family history. My first try at a title for my biography of Mary Kirkpatrick was firmly of this variety: *Mary Kirkptrick: Matriarch of the Macleay.*

As you write and become more confident with the family history, a title can emerge that exemplifies the main themes. A title is often taken from an anecdote or quote in a letter or other document. At other times the best strategy is to choose a simple description of the main story such as Mary McCarthy's *Memories of a Catholic Childhood* or Brian Matthew's *Louisa* (a biography of Louisa Lawson).

The final title I chose for my biography of Mary Kirkpatrick was *Memories & Dreams: A Biography of Nurse Mary Kirkpatrick*. The main title reflected how memory and oral history were used in the book and the subtitle simply states what the book is about.

Author obligations—referencing

There are two reasons for referencing: one is to provide an aid for readers and other researchers using your book and also to meet your obligations as a historian; the second reason relates to plagiarism and the need to acknowledge other people's work and, at times, to obtain permission to reproduce it.

Throughout the text, you should reference your sources of information as you proceed to write the story. For example, if you record that your great grandfather arrived in Australia in 1841 on the ship *Cambodia* accompanied by his brother, that their country of origin was Ireland and then list their occupations and their parents' names, you should use a footnote, endnote or textual reference to show where the information was obtained. The full reference is then given in a bibliography at the end of the book.

Footnotes

Readers are directed to a footnote by a superscript number or symbol placed either at a relevant point in the text or at the end of a sentence. This number or symbol directs readers to a corresponding note at the bottom of the page. The note may expand on a certain point or enable the reader to identify and locate the source of information or specific work referred to in the text. Footnotes should provide sufficient information for this purpose. Consistency in presentation should be maintained.

Following is an example of how footnotes are used:

The care and education of very young children has always been seen as the special province of women.[1] In private and state schools, women were employed to work with children considered too young for primary or elementary schooling.[2] Infant and Dame Schools were usually opened by women and although older children might attend, such schools were viewed as essentially dealing with elementary schooling of a very rudimentary kind.[3]

---

1   N. Kyle, *Her Natural Destiny: The Education of Women in New South Wales*, New South Wales University Press, Kensington, 1986, pp. 1–10.
2   H. Jones, *Nothing Seemed Impossible: Women's Education and Social Change in South Australia*, University of Queensland Press, St Lucia, 1985.
3   A. Barcan, *A Short History of Education in New South Wales*, Martindale Press, Sydney, 1965, pp. 61–6.

Using footnotes for additional information is common in traditional history journals and books. Peruse the shelves of a reference library and compare how different texts and authors use referencing styles. For example:

This was now Mary Carpenter's great object. It was inevitable, as she knew, that a long time must elapse before any scheme found on the report of the Committee could secure Parliamentary sanction.[1] Meanwhile she became more and more anxious to prove the correctness of the views and the feasibility of the proposals which she had urged.

[1]   The dissolution of Parliament did in fact bring its sittings to a close in the summer of 1852. The evidence so collected was published in a special Blue Book, without any report from the Committee. The proceedings were renewed under a new Committee (of nearly the same composition as the old) after the first meeting of Parliament in November; but the recommendations of the Committee were not issued until the summer of 1853.

Footnotes collected at the bottom of each page are distracting for the reader. If something is worth writing about, include it in the main text. Distracting readers with long, tedious footnotes is outdated and unnecessary. Wherever possible, use endnotes or text references for citing your sources instead of footnotes.

Endnotes

Endnotes are used for referencing, and are cited in the same way as footnotes but are collected at the end of each chapter or at the end of the title.

Superscript numbers are used to indicate endnotes in the text, beginning at '1' for each chapter.

Textual reference

A textual reference (usually the Harvard author–date system) can be used instead of footnotes or endnotes for referencing of sources. Full details of sources are then listed in a bibliography at the end of the title. For example:

> The care and education of very young children has always been seen as the special province of women (Kyle 1986, pp. 1–10). In private and state schools women were employed to work with children considered too young for primary or elementary schooling (Jones 1985; Henry 1982; Smith 1943). Infant and Dame Schools were usually opened by women and although older children might attend, such schools were viewed as essentially dealing with elementary schooling of a very rudimentary kind (Barcan 1965, pp. 61–6).

Citing your sources

The first rule of citation is consistency. If in doubt about how to reference, your aim should be to facilitate your reader's capacity to find the source if they wish to do further research. Thus, simplicity, clarity and accuracy are your key objectives. Elizabeth Shown Mills, *Evidence! Citation and Analysis for the Family Historian* is a useful guide for family historians, as is Richard Lackey's *Cite Your Sources*. The *AGPS Style Manual: For authors, editors and printers* has a detailed chapter titled, 'Methods of citation', and includes advice on citing from new technologies such as video, television and electronic material (email, websites, CD-ROMs, electronic databases).

Books

In a footnote or endnote reference, the accepted sequence has the initial placed first then the surname, title of the book, publisher, where published, year published and page number(s) where the particular information is located:

1   B. Kingston, *My Wife, My Daughter and Poor Mary Ann: Women and Work in Australia*, Nelson, Melbourne, 1975, p. 4.

Articles

For articles, the initial is placed first followed by the surname, (unlike in the bibliography, where the surname is placed first, see p. 263) name of article, journal name, volume and number, year and page number:

F. Chan, 'Papua New Guinea Records', *Your Family Tree*, vol. 1, no. 5, 1987, p. 9.

Government publications

With this kind of reference, the first rule is to include as much information as will make it possible for the reader to locate the source document. Government publications vary considerably in their scope and where they can be accessed by the researcher. You will need to use your judgement about each one as you construct your footnotes, endnotes or textual references. For example:

> New South Wales, *Parliamentary Debates*, First Series, vol.
> XXXI, 25 June 1892, pp. 2173–78.
> Colonial Secretary, Letters Received Special Bundles,
> 1826–1963, Folio 63, Series H3256, New South Wales
> State Records (NSWSR).
> Department of Public Instruction, *Annual Reports*,
> 1880–1920, Government Printer, Sydney.

Manuscripts or family papers

Nothing is underlined, italicised or placed in bold type when citing unpublished manuscript material or family papers. Include the library's title of the collection and any library identification number/s. For example:

> Dallas, Stewart, and Steel Family Papers, MSS 1218, Mitchell
> Library, New South Wales State Library.
> Parkes to T.T. Ewing, 2 May 1891, Parkes Correspondence,
> Mitchell Library, MSS A907, p. 31.
> Jones, J. R., Birth Certificate, Registry of Birth, Deaths and
> Marriages NSW, in the possession of the author.

Newspapers

> *Sydney Morning Herald*, 19 May 1832, pp. 4–6.
> *Illawarra Mercury*, 10 June 1892, p. 12.

> Even if you do decide to do things differently from the standard referencing conventions, it is most important that you observe two fundamental rules:
>
> • Provide enough information in a footnote, endnote or bibliography for a reader to be able to locate your source.
> • Be consistent throughout the entire book once you have decided upon a suitable convention to follow.

Bibliographies

A bibliography is a complete list of all of the sources cited in the text whether they be primary or secondary sources. All books, documents, reports, newspapers, letters, wills, certificates and diaries are listed. In the case of primary source material, the actual location of the material is listed as well. Family historians should attach a bibliography, even if not required for referencing, so that their readers, especially other family members and local historians, can locate material they might want to make use of.

A bibliography usually appears at the end of a book, with all entries listed in alphabetical order. Unlike with footnotes or endnotes, all sources cited begin with the surname of the author or with the significant name or phrase in a title so that they are easily identified in an alphabetical list.

The use of endnotes is said to make a bibliography less necessary these days. You might choose to have a select list for the bibliography, organised as follows:

Primary sources

Manuscript collections (includes family letters, certificates, official manuscripts from libraries and archives)

Colonial Secretary, Letters Received Special Bundles, 1826–1965, Archives Office of New South Wales

Newcastle School of Arts Minute Books, 1880–1929, Newcastle Public Library

Public bodies and local authorities, papers and printed reports

University of Sydney, Manual of Public Examinations, 1878–1912, Fisher Library, University of Sydney

Voluntary societies, papers and printed papers

Parliamentary papers

Queensland, 'Votes & Proceedings'

Family publications, including bibles, cookbooks, diaries, and family papers

Dallas, Stewart, and Steel Family Papers, Mitchell Library, MSS 1218

Journals, magazines, directories, newspapers and pamphlets

Le Feuilleton (Claremont college magazine), vol. 1, no. 2, 1905–1909.

Moores Australian Almanac and Country Directory, 1873–1905.

Oral interviews
Interview with A. Smith, 8/10/92, letter/transcript in possession of the author.

Letters and emails
Letter from Kathleen Laney to Noeline Kyle, 7 May 1978.

Secondary sources
Theses
Hone, A., 1963, 'The Movement of Higher Education for Women in Victoria in the Nineteenth Century', MA Thesis, Monash University.

Articles and conference papers
Cleverley, J., 1964, 'Tutors and Governesses in Australian Literature', *Education*, vol. 45, no. 5, p. 3.

Books
Crowley, F. (ed.) 1976, *A New History of Australia*, Heinemann, Melbourne.
Twopeny, R. E. N., 1973, *Town Life in Australia*, facsimile edition, Sydney University Press (first published 1883).

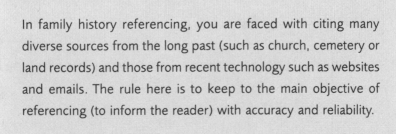

In family history referencing, you are faced with citing many diverse sources from the long past (such as church, cemetery or land records) and those from recent technology such as websites and emails. The rule here is to keep to the main objective of referencing (to inform the reader) with accuracy and reliability.

Indexes

Your family history will have more value as history if you provide an index. In your index include the names of men, women and children, maiden names cross-referenced with married names, place names, names of ships, ports, districts, regions and/or countries, occupations, organisations, major themes such as immigration, economic downturns or depressions, convicts and transportation, births, deaths, marriages, children's games and leisure activities, divorce, criminal details, overseas origins, punishment, local history, transport and communication, housing and living conditions.

It is not much use compiling your index until you have a final manuscript, that is, the version that goes to your printer. Constructing an index and correcting it in proof pages is a time-consuming and complex job but will be well worth it. Alternatively, you can utilise the services of a professional indexer to create an index for your title, although this can be a relatively expensive option.

The business of publishing

Many first-time authors, especially if they are self-publishing, feel intimidated by the many procedures involved in getting a book into print. However, there are many references on publishing available to guide you, such as the *AGPS Style*

Manual: For authors, editors and printers. The following list of items should help get you started.

Legal deposit

You are required under the copyright act and various state acts to deposit a copy of your book in the National Library of Australia and the State Library in which you live. You should do this as soon as possible after publication. The website for legal deposit is <http://www.nla.gov.au/services/deposit.html>.

Lending rights

Public Lending Right (PLR) is a scheme whereby publishers, writers and creators are compensated for the number of their books held in Australian public libraries. You must have at least 50 copies of your book in Australian public libraries to receive a PLR payment each year. If you receive royalties or are a publisher and an Australian citizen, you are eligible for PLR.

Education Lending Right (ELR) is compensation for books held in school, university and other educational institutions. ELR is not as relevant for family history but it's worthwhile registering your book anyway.

It is free to register your book for PLR and ELR and once registered it is registered for life. You can find out the details at the website <http://www.dcita.gov.au/lendingrights>.

International Standard Book Number

The 10-digit International Standard Book Number (ISBN) enables libraries and booksellers to identify your book more easily, and simplifies the book ordering process. It is administered by D.W. Thorpe.

You can purchase a single ISBN number in Australia for $33 plus a new publisher registration fee of $44. Or you can, if you think you will be publishing more books, buy a block of ten numbers for $69.50 plus the $44 for new publishers.

You can obtain the application form from the website <http://www.thorpe.com.au> or contact D.W. Thorpe via email at <isbn.agency@thorpe.com.au>.

Barcode

At the same time as you obtain your ISBN from D.W. Thorpe, you can order a barcode. The cost is $38 per ISBN. A barcode can facilitate management of your book for bookshops, libraries and in other repositories. D.W. Thorpe will deliver the barcode via email and you can forward it to your printer.

Cataloguing in Publication

Cataloguing in Publication (CIP) is a free service administered by the National Library of Australia. Registering with CIP will ensure that your book will be on their database and have a wider audience. Check CIP details at the website <http://www.nla.gov.au/services/CIP.html>.

Australian books in print

To distribute your book details to a wider range of distributors, libraries and other organisations, D.W. Thorpe offers a free service, listing your book under their Australian Books in Print. Email them at <infoservies@thorpe.com.au> or check their website at <http://www.thorpe.com.au>.

Marketing, distribution and promotion

Unless you have prospects of sales apart from the family or the local community, stay away from expensive marketing and distribution. Some key strategies for promoting and selling a family history are:

- Involve as many people from the family as possible in the family history. When your family see their names are in print, hopefully this will encourage them to buy it. Ensure, however, that you have permission to print all names.
- Link your launch to a family reunion. You can include the price in the attendance fee, perhaps with a refund guaranteed if they do not like it.
- A book launch is a significant expense. However, in the case of family history, it may be worthwhile. Plan your launch in a central location for the family. The local area where the family lived and worked is a good choice. Ask

a local personality to launch it for you and invite family, friends, community members and local identities.

- Using a distributor for your book is not worthwhile unless your book has a wider audience than the family. Retailers and other organisations will take a big percentage, usually 40 to 60 per cent, leaving you with little profit. Direct sales are your main selling avenue.

- If you decide to place your book with a bookshop, try library bookshops, genealogical bookshops, museum bookshops and small outlets that are more likely to take your book on consignment and also with less commission.

- You can sell your book through a website, although most experience of this suggests that sales are few.

- Public libraries and school libraries may buy copies. List your book with the library-buying network of Bennett Pty Ltd, the major library buyers in Australia. Their website is <http://www.bennett.com.au/>.

- Your best market is your family and the local community. Organise free publicity in local newspapers and on local radio stations. Ask to do a talk at the local library or family history society, and always take a few books with you wherever you go. You never know when you can sell just one or two.

- Design a flyer and email it to as many organisations, local libraries, individuals or relevant societies as you think will be interested. Even if only a few sales result, it is worth it as emailing is less costly than postage. However, you might have to mail a few and bear the cost if you think it worthwhile.

- Send free copies of your book to libraries or societies you have used for research and also to other organisations that might promote your book. Also send free copies to a local newspaper or family history society and to the Society of Australian Genealogists, and ask for a review of it in the next edition of their journal.

EXERCISES

- White space is important in page design. Study magazine layouts and note their use of white space. Examine recent published family history (try to choose those with many illustrations and photographs); check how white space helps the reader and how you might improve on or perhaps copy the techniques being used.

- Organise a talk at a local family history group or other organisation in the area where your ancestors once lived. Ask if you can talk to friends of the local library or write a summary of your book for the local newspaper.

- Study the way in which published family histories are produced. Look at the contents page, foreword and the title pages. Are the photographs, maps and illustrations well placed? Do captions give useful information and are the individuals named clearly and appropriately?

- Carefully check all footnotes and referencing to ensure the correctness of your work.
- Have you presented the family history in a logical sequence? Check how sections and paragraphs flow. Have you used white space and positioned photographs in the best possible way?

NOTES

Chapter 1

1   T. Binning, 'Heart Songs in the Dandenongs' in *Remembering Mothers: An inspiring anthology of short stories, letters and poetry*, (eds) N. Kyle et al, Northern Rivers Family History Writers' Group, Alstonville, 2005, p. 128.
2   N. Kyle, *Memories & Dreams: A Biography of Nurse Mary Kirkpatrick*, the author, Mullumbimby, 2001, p. 11.
3   Y. Hammond, 'Cradle to the Grave' in *Remembering Mothers*, pp. 36–7.
4   J. Chang, *Wild Swans: Three Daughters of China*, Flamingo, 1992.

Chapter 2

1   Cited in D. Lowenthal, *The Past is a Foreign Country*, Cambridge University Press, Oxford, 1985, p. 193.
2   P. Clarke, *A Colonial Woman: The life and times of Mary Braidwood Mowle*, Allen & Unwin, Sydney, 1986.
3   N. Kyle, 'I'll take you home Kathleen...' in *Remembering Mothers: An inspiring anthology of short stories, letters and poetry*, (eds) N.

Kyle et al, Northern Rivers Family History Writers' Group, Alstonville, 2005, pp. 151–63.

4   N. Kyle, 'I'll take you home Kathleen...', op cit, pp. 162–3.

5   D. Lowenthal, *The Past is a Foreign Country*, p. 215, my emphasis.

Chapter 3

1   D. Simson, *Caroline's Story: The story of the Miskin family of Kent in Queensland*, the author, Brisbane, 1997 p. 1.

Chapter 4

1   N. Kyle, *Memories & Dreams: A Biography of Nurse Mary Kirkpatrick*, the author, Mullumbimby, 2001, p. 7.

2   N. Kyle, *Memories & Dreams*, pp. 7–8.

Chapter 5

1   G. Davison and C. McConville (eds) *A Heritage Handbook*, Allen & Unwin, Sydney, 1988.

2   B. James, *No Man's Land: Women of the Northern Territory*, Collins, Sydney, 1989, p. 49.

3   B. Berzins, *North Coast Women: A History to 1939*, Royal Australian Historical Society, Sydney, 1996, pp. 48–9.

4   G. Davison and C. McConville, op. cit.

5   A.G. Thomson Zain'uddin, 'Rose Inagaki: Is It a Crime To Marry a Foreigner?' in *Double Time: Women in Victoria—150 years*, eds M. Lake and F. Kelly, Penguin Books, Australia Ltd., Ringwood, 1985, p. 335.

6   Cited in A.G. Thomson Zain'uddin, 'Rose Inagaki', ibid.

7   ibid.

Chapter 6

1 R. Siemon, *The Mayne Inheritance*, University of Queensland Press, St Lucia, 2001, p. 15.
2 D. Cox, 'Not All Plain Sailing' in *Remembering Mothers: An inspiring anthology of short stories, letters and poetry*, (eds) N. Kyle et al, Northern Rivers Family History Writers' Group, Alstonville, 2001, p. 86.
3 B. Worthington, 'What is a "Mother"?' in *Remembering Mothers*, p. 104.
4 J. Bardon and D. Burnett, *Belfast: A Pocket History*, The Blackstaff Press, Belfast, 1996, pp. 72–3.
5 N. Kyle, *Memories & Dreams: A Biography of Nurse Mary Kirkpatrick*, the author, Mullumbimby, 2001, p. 13.
6 E. McDonald, 'George Brown and Bethice Noble', unpublished story.

Chapter 8

1 L.P. Gouldrup, *Writing the Family Narrative*, Ancestry Incorporated, 1987, pp. 64–5.
2 ibid.
3 L. Semple, 'Never in a Mother of Sundays' in *Remembering Mothers: An inspiring anthology of short stories, letters and poetry*, (eds) N. Kyle et al, Northern Rivers Family History Writers' Group, Alstonville, 2001, p. 15.
4 N. Kyle, *Memories & Dreams: A Biography of Nurse Mary Kirkpatrick*, the author, Mullumbimby, 2001, p. 103.
5 J. Gracie Mulcahy, 'She Had a Wicked Wit' in *Remembering Mothers*, pp. 27–8.
6 C. Kempthorne, *For All Time: A Complete Guide to Writing Your Family History*, Boynton/Cook Publishers, Heinemann, Portsmouth, 1996, pp. 36–7.
7 Biography Assistant Help, <http://www.genealogy.com/bio/index/html>.
8 H. Edwards, *Writing a Non-boring Family History*, Hale & Iremonger, Sydney, 2003, pp. 59–62.
9 N. Kyle, *Memories & Dreams*, p. 12.

10 B.K. Garis, '1890–1900', in F. Crowley (ed.), *A New History of Australia*, William Heinemann, Melbourne, 1976, p. 247.

11 J.F.C. Harrison, *The Common People: A History from the Norman Conquest to the Present*, Flamingo, 1984, p. 303.

12 Gouldrup, *Writing the Family Narrative*, pp. 147–8.

13 S. Szeman, *Mastering Point of View: How to control point of view to create, conflict, depth and suspense*, Story Press, Cincinnati, 2001, p. 26.

14 R. Holmes, *Footsteps: Adventures of a Romantic Biographer*, Penguin Books Australia, Ringwood, 1986, p. 97.

15 H. Holmes, 'She was Delicate but Strong, like a Bone China Cup', in *Remembering Mothers*, p. 54.

16 ibid., p. 69.

Chapter 9

1 A.G.L. Shaw, '1788–1810' in *A New History of Australia*, (ed.) F. Crowley, William Heinemann, Melbourne, p. 1.

2 L. Douglas and P. Spearritt, 'Talking History: The Use of Oral Sources' in *New History: Studying Australia Today*, (eds) F. Osborne and W.F. Mandle, Allen & Unwin, Sydney, 1982, p. 51.

3 R. Siemon, *The Mayne Inheritance*, University of Queensland Press, St Lucia, 1999, p. xi.

4 W. Strunk, Jr. and E.B. White, *The Elements of Style*, MacMillan, London.

5 ibid., pp. 60–1.

6 *Style Manual: For authors, editors and printers*, revised by Snooks & Co., John Wiley & Sons Australia, 6th edition, 2002, pp. 55–62.

7 N. Kyle, *Memories & Dreams: A biography of Nurse Mary Kirkpatrick*, the author, Mullumbimby, 2001, p. 111.

8 D.G. Bowd, *Hawkesbury Journey: Up the Windsor Road from Baulkham Hills*, Library of Australian History, Sydney, 1994, pp. 60–2.

9 ibid.

10 ibid., p. 61.

11 ibid.

12 D. Modjeska, *Poppy*, McPhee Gribble/Penguin Books, Ringwood, 1990, p. 93.
13 ibid., p. 317.
14 ibid.

Chapter 10

1 N. Kyle, 'Just Imagine', *Queensland Family Historian*, vol. 20, no. 4, November, 1999, pp. 123–4.
2 N. Kyle, *Memories & Dreams: A Biography of Nurse Mary Kirkpatrick*, the author, Mullumbimby, 2001, p. 105.
3 D. Montgomery, 'The Music Teacher and the Milkman', unpublished story.
4 A. McGrath, 'Spinifex Fairies: Aboriginal workers in the Northern Territory, 1911–39', in E. Windschuttle (ed.), *Women, Class and History: Feminist Perspectives on Australia 1788–1978*, Fontana/Collins, Sydney, 1980, pp. 237–58.

Chapter 12

1 C. Cordner, *A Mavis Singing: The Story of an Australian Family*, New South Wales University Press, Kensington, 1986, p. 1.

Chapter 13

1 E. Mitchell, *Self-Publishing Made Simple; The Ultimate Australian Guide*, Hardie Grant Books, South Yarra, 2000, pp. 53–66.

BIBLIOGRAPHY AND RESOURCES

Family history research

Bateson, C., *The Convict Ships, 1787–1868*, Library of Australian History, Sydney, 1983

Borchardt, D.H., *Checklist of Royal Commissions, Select Committees of Parliament and Boards of Inquiry, Part IV, New South Wales, 1855–1960*, La Trobe University Library, Bundoora, 1975

Burgman, V. and Lee, J. (eds), A *Most Valuable Acquisition: A People's History of Australia Since 1788*, McPhee Gribble/Penguin Books Australia, Ringwood, 1988

Burgman, V. and Lee, J., *Constructing a Culture: A People's History of Australia since 1788*, McPhee Gribble/Penguin Books Australia, Ringwood, 1988

Burgman, V. and Lee, J., *Staining the Wattle: A People's History of Australia since 1788*, McPhee Gribble/Penguin Books Australia, Ringwood, 1988

Charlwood, D., *The Long Farewell: The Perilous Voyages of Settlers Under Sail in the Great Migrations to Australia*, Penguin Books, Ringwood, 1981

Christian, P., *The Genealogist's Internet*, National Archives, Kew, 2005

Crowley, F. (ed.), *A New History of Australia*, William Heinemann, Melbourne, 1976

Eslick, C., Hughes, J. and Jack, R.I., *Bibliography of New South Wales Local History*, New South Wales University Press, Kensington, 1987

Foley, C. and Lynch, R., *The History of Leisure in Australia: A Bibliography*, online bibliography no. 3, School of Leisure, Sport & Tourism, University of Technology Sydney, 1994 at <www.business.uts.edu.au /lst/research/bibliographies.html>

Gray, N., *Compiling Your Family History*, ABC Enterprises & Society of Australian Genealogists, Sydney, 1996

Hibbins, G.M., Fahey, C., and Askew, M.R., *Local History: A Handbook for Enthusiasts*, Allen & Unwin, Sydney, 1985

Hughes, J.N., *Local Government . . . Local History: A guide to N.S.W. Local Government Minute Books and Rate Records*, Royal Australian Historical Society, Sydney, 1990

Hughes, J.N., *New South Wales Directories 1828–1950: A Bibliography*, New South Wales University Press, Kensington, 1987

Kane, E., *Doing Your Own Research: How to do basic descriptive research in the social sciences and the humanities*, Marion Bayers, London, 1987

Kyle, N. and King, R., *The Family History Writing Book*, Allen & Unwin, Sydney, 1993

Kyle, N., *Tracing Family History in Australia*, Methuen, Sydney, 1985

Lowenthal, D., *The Past is a Foreign Country*, Cambridge University Press, Cambridge, 1983

Mackinolty J. (ed.), *Past Continuous: Learning Through the Historical Environment*, History Teachers' Association of Australia, Rozelle, Sydney, 1983

McClaughlin, T., *From Shamrock to Wattle: Digging Up Your Irish Ancestors*, Collins, Sydney, 1985

Nunn, C., *Websites for Genealogists*, the author, Pearce, ACT, 1998

Osborne, G. and Mandle, W.F. (eds), *New History: Studying Australia Today*, George Allen & Unwin, Sydney, 1982

St Leon, M., *Spangles & Sawdust: The Circus in Australia*, Greenhouse Publications, Melbourne, 1983

Vine Hall, N., *Tracing Your Family History in Australia: A national guide to sources*, the author, Albert Park, 2002

Oral history, public history and heritage

Ashton, P., *On the Record: A practical guide to oral history*, A Cultural Initiative of North Sydney Council, North Sydney Municipal Council, North Sydney, 1991

Breakwell, G.M., *Interviewing: Problems in Practice*, BPS Books & Routledge, Leicester, 1990

Cullen, P., *Looking Locally: A Local Studies Resources Package*, Queensland Department of Education, Darling Downs Region, Toowoomba, 1988

Davison, G. and McConville, C. (eds), *A Heritage Handbook*, Allen & Unwin, Sydney, 1991

Dymond, D., *Writing Local History*, British Association for Local History & Phillimore, Sussex, 1988

Minichiello, V., Aroni, R., Timewell, E. and Alexander, L., *In-Depth Interviewing: Researching People*, Longman Cheshire, Melbourne, 1990

Robertson, B., *Oral History: A Handbook*, Oral History Association of Australia, Unley, 2006.

White, O., Schwirtlich, A. and Nash, J., *Our Heritage: A Directory of Archives and Manuscript Repositories in Australia*, Australian Society of Archives, O'Connor, 1983

Writing family history

Barrington, J., *Writing the Memoir*, Allen & Unwin, Sydney, 1997

Bates, D., *The New Writer's Survival Guide: An Introduction to the Craft of Writing*, Penguin, Ringwood, 1990

Beazley, M. and Marr, G., *The Writer's Handbook*, Phoenix Education, Albert Park, 1996

Berry, L., *Writing and Publishing Your Family History*, Lesle Berry, Blackburn, 2005

Cameron, J., *The Artist's Way: A Spiritual Path to Higher Creativity*, Pan Books, London, 1994

Donovan, P., *So, You Want to Write History?*, Donovan & Associates, Blackwood, 1992

Dunn, I., *The Writer's Guide: A companion to writing for pleasure or publication*, Allen & Unwin, Sydney, 2002

Edwards, H., *Writing a 'Non-boring' Family History*, Hale & Iremonger, Sydney, 1997

Fine Clouse, B., *265 Troubleshooting Strategies for Writing Nonfiction*, McGraw-Hill, New York, 2005

Gee, P., *The Story of Your Life: How to Stop Stalling and Start Writing*, Debut Publishing, Brisbane, 1999

Gouldrup, L.P., *Writing the Family Narrative*, Ancestry Incorporated, 1987

Gray, N., *Compiling Your Family History*, ABC Enterprises & the Society of Australian Genealogists, Sydney, 1989

Grenville, K., *The Writing Book: A Workbook for Fiction Writers*, Allen & Unwin, Sydney, 1990

Jamieson, A., *Creative Writing: Researching, Planning & Writing for Publication*, Focal Press, Oxford, 1996

Kempthorne, C., *For All Time: A Complete Guide to Writing Your Family History*, Baynton/Cook Publishers, Portsmouth, 1996

Ledoux, D., *Turning Memories into Memoirs: A Handbook for Writing Lifestories*, Soliel Press, Lisbon Falls, Maine, 1993

Meadley, D., *Writing a Family History*, Australian Institute of Genealogical Studies, Oakleigh, 1985

Miller. P., *Writing Your Life: A Journey of Discovery*, Allen & Unwin, Sydney, 1984

Methold, K., *A–Z of Authorship: A Professional Guide*, Keesing Press & Australian Society of Authors, Sydney, 1996

Murphy, E., *You Can Write: A Do-it-Yourself Manual*, Longman Cheshire, Melbourne, 1985

Polking, K., *Writing Family Histories and Memories*, Betterway Books, Cincinnatti, 1995

Robertson, H., *Writing From Life: A Guide for Writing True Stories*, McClelland & Stewart Inc., Toronto, 1998

Rosier-Jones, J., *So You Want to Write: A Practical & Inspirational Guide*, Tandem Press, Buckland, 2000

Schwarz, S., *Australian Guide to Getting Published*, Hale & Iremonger, Sydney, 1995

Writing about the family and children

Aries, P., *Centuries of Childhood*, Penguin Books, Jonathan Cape, London, 1960

Burns, A. and Goodnow, J., *Children & Families in Australia*, Allen & Unwin, Sydney, 1979

Burns, A., Bottomley, G. and Jools, P. (eds), *The Family in the Modern World*, Allen & Unwin, Sydney, 1983

Fabian, S. and Loh, M., *Children in Australia: An Outline History*, rev. edn, Oxford University Press, Melbourne, 1980

Funder, K., *Images of Australian Families: Approaches and Perspectives*, Longman Cheshire, Melbourne, 1991

Gilding, M., *The Making and Breaking of the Australian Family*, Allen & Unwin, Sydney, 1991

Grimshaw, P., McConville, C. and McEwen, E. (eds), *Families in Colonial Australia*, Allen & Unwin, Sydney, 1985

Humphries, S., Mack, J. and Perks, R., *A Century of Childhood*, Sidgwick & Jackson, London, 1988

Kociumbas, J., *Australian Childhood: A History*, Allen & Unwin, Sydney, 1997

Kyle, N., *Her Natural Destiny: The Education of Women in New South Wales*, New South Wales University Press, Kensington, 1986

Ramsland, J., *Children of the Backlanes: Destitute and Neglected Children in Colonial New South Wales*, New South Wales University Press, Kensington, 1986

Reiger, K.M., *The Disenchantment of the Home: Modernising the Australian Family 1880–1940*, Oxford University Press, Melbourne, 1985

Shorter, E., *The Making of the Modern Family*, Fontana/Collins, London, 1977

Townsend, H., *Baby Boomers: Growing up in Australia in the 1940s, 50s and 60s*, Simon & Schuster, Brookvale, 1988

Van Krieken, R., *Children and the State: Social Control and the Formation of Australian Child Welfare*, Allen & Unwin, Sydney, 1991

Walvin, J., *A Child's World: A Social History of English Childhood 1800–1914*, Penguin, Ringwood, 1982

Writing about women

Alford, K., *Production or reproduction? An economic history of women in Australia, 1788–1850*, Oxford University Press, Melbourne, 1984

Beddoe, D., *Welsh Convict Women: A Study of Women Transported from Wales to Australia, 1787–1852*, S. Williams, Barry, 1979

Berzins, B., *North Coast Women: A History to 1939*, Royal Australian Historical Society, Sydney, 1996

Brock, P. (ed.), *Women Rites and Sites: Aboriginal Women's Cultural Knowledge*, Allen & Unwin, Sydney, 1989

Daniels, K., *Convict Women*, Allen & Unwin, Sydney, 1998

Daniels, K. and Murnane, M. (eds), *Uphill all the Way: A Documentary History of Women in Australia*, University of Queensland Press, St Lucia, 1980

DeBartolo Carmack, S., *A Genealogist's Guide to Discovering Your Female Ancestors*, Betterway Books, Cincinnati, 1998

Dixson, M., *The Real Matilda: Woman and Identity in Australia 1788 to 1975*, Penguin Books, Ringwood, 1976

Frost, L., *Searching for Mary Ann: Researching Women Ancestors in Australia*, the author, Essendon, 1994

Gothard, J., *Blue China: Single Female Migration to Colonial Australia*, Melbourne University Press, Melbourne, 2001

Grimshaw, P., Lake, M., McGrath, A. and Quartly, M., *Creating a Nation: 1788–1990*, McPhee Gribble Publishers, Ringwood, 1994

Kingston, B., *The World Moves Slowly: A Documentary History of Australian Women*, Cassell Australia, Stanmore, 1977

Kingston, B., *My Wife, My Daughter and Poor Mary Ann: Women and Work in Australia*, Nelson, Melbourne, 1975

Kyle, N., *We Should've Listened to Grandma: Women and Family History*, Allen & Unwin, Sydney, 1988

McClaughlin, T., *Barefoot and Pregnant: Irish Famine Orphans In Australia*, vol. 1 and vol. 2, The Genealogical Society of Victoria, Melbourne, 1991

Mackinolty, J. and Radi, H. (eds), *In Pursuit of Justice: Australian Women and the Law 1788–1979*, Hale & Iremonger, Sydney, 1979

Mercer, J. (ed.), *The Other Half: Women in Australian Society*, Penguin Books, Ringwood, 1975

Oxley, D., *Convict Maids: The forced migration of women to Australia*, Cambridge University Press, Cambridge, 1996

Pownall, E., *Mary of Maranoa: Tales of Australian Pioneer Women*, F.H. Johnston, Sydney, 1959

Radi, H. (ed.), *200 Australian Women: a Redress anthology*, Women's Redress Press, Broadway, 1988

Richards, E. (ed.), *Visible Women: Female Immigrants in Colonial Australia*, Research School of Social Sciences, Australian National University, Canberra, 1995

Robinson, P., *The Women of Botany Bay: A reinterpretation of the role of women in the origins of Australian society*, The Macquarie Library, Sydney, 1988

Salt, A., *These Outcast Women: The Parramatta Female Factory, 1821–1848*, Hale & Iremonger, Sydney, 1984

Schaffer, K., *Women and the Bush: Forces of Desire in the Australian Cultural Tradition*, Cambridge University Press, Cambridge, 1988

Summers, A., *Damned Whores and God's Police: The Colonisation of Women in Australia*, Penguin, Ringwood, 1975

Teale, R. (ed.), *Colonial Eve: Sources on women in Australia 1788–1914*, Oxford University Press, Melbourne, 1978

Thompson, P. and Yorke, S. (eds), *Lives Obscurely Great: Historical Essays on Women of New South Wales*, Society of Women Writers (Australia), New South Wales Branch, Sydney, 1981

Theobald, M., *Knowing Women: Origins of Women's Education*, Cambridge University Press, Cambridge, 1996

Editing, word usage and publishing

Beaumont, J., *How to Write and Publish Your Family History*, Orlando Press, Sydney, 1985

Clark, S., *Successful Self-Publishing: Marketing and Selling Your Own Book*, Hale & Iremonger, Sydney, 1997

Field, M., *The Writer's Guide to Research: An invaluable guide to gathering material for features, novels and non-fiction books*, How to Books, Oxford, 2000

Foord, K. (ed.), *Publish: A Writer's Handbook*, Arts Council of the ACT Inc., Canberra, 1991

Hale & Iremonger, *Guide to Book Production: A step-by-step guide to successful and cost-effective book production*, Hale & Iremonger, Sydney, 2000

Hornadge, B., *How to Publish Your Own Book: A Complete Guide to Self-Publishing in Australia*, Review Publications, Dubbo, 1986

Kaplan, B., *Editing Made Easy*, Penguin, Camberwell, 2003

Kaplan, C., *Publish for Profit: How to Write, Market & Promote Your Own Book*, the author, Bellevue Hill, 1997

Mitchell, E., *Self-Publishing Made Simple: The Ultimate Australian Guide*, Hardie Grant Books, South Yarra, 2000

Murray-Smith, S., *Right Words: A Guide to English Usage in Australia*, Penguin, Ringwood, 1990

Phillips, A., *Desktop Publishing for Family Historians*, Gould Books, Gumeracha, 1990

Poynter, D., *The Self-Publishing Manual: How to Write, Print and Sell Your Own Book*, 9th edn, Para Publishing, Santa Barbara, 1996

Ross-Larson, B., *Edit Yourself: A manual for everyone who works with words*, W.W. Norton & Company, New York, 1996

Schwarz, S., *Australian Guide to Getting Published*, Hale & Iremonger, Sydney, 1995

Stacpole, J., *Publish It Yourself: A comprehensive guide to writing and self-publishing non-fiction*, John Maxwell & Associates, North Balwyn, 1999

Style Manual: For authors, editors and printers, revised by Snooks & Co., 6th edn, John Wiley & Sons Australia, Ltd., Melbourne, 2002

Whitton, R. (ed.), *The Australian Writer's Marketplace 2000: The Complete Guide to Being Published in Australia*, Bookman, Melbourne, 2000
Whitton, R. and Hollingworth, S., *A Decent Proposal: How to Sell Your Book to an Australian Publisher*, Common Ground, Altona, 2001

Author obligations, citing sources, referencing and bibliographies

Books

Ferris Curran, J., *Numbering Your Genealogy: Sound and Simple Systems*, National Genealogical Society, Arlington, Virginia (special publication no. 59), 1992
Lackey, R.S., *Cite Your Sources: A Manual for Documenting Family Histories and Genealogical Records*, University of Mississippi Press, Jackson, 1980
Shown Mills, E., *Evidence! Citation & Analysis for the Family Historian*, Genealogical Publishing Company, Baltimore, 1997
State Library of New South Wales, *Coping with Copyright: A Guide to Using Pictorial and Written Material in Australian Libraries and Archives*, State Library of NSW Press, Sydney, 1991
Strunk, W. and White, E.B., *The Elements of Style*, MacMillan, London, 1972
Strunk's Elements of Style, full online version, plus Fowler, H.W., *The King's English*, 2nd edn, 1908; *Roget's II: The New Thesaurus*, 3rd edn, 1995; and *Columbia Encyclopaedia*, 6th edn, 2001, at the following website maintained by Bartleby.com: <http://www.bartleby.com/141/>
Venolia, J., *Write Right: A Desktop Digest of Punctuation, Grammar and Style*, Ten Speed Press/Periwinkle Press, Berkeley, California, 1995

Websites

Copyright:
Australian Copyright Council have free information sheets on their website, including: Copying photographs you pay for (G35); Maps

and charts (G090); Duration of copyright (G23); Family histories
and copyright (G042); Quotes and extracts (G34); Databases,
compilations, tables and forms (G66).
Australian Copyright Council
PO Box 1986
Strawberry Hills NSW 2012
Australia
245 Chalmers Street
Redfern NSW 2016
Australia
Fax: (02) 9698 3536
<http://www.copyright.org.au/specialinterest/writing.htm>
Copyright (USA): <http://www.copyright.gov/>
Cataloguing-in-Publication (CIP) Australia:
Cataloguing-in-Publication Unit
National Library of Australia
Canberra ACT 2600
Phone: (02) 6262 1458
<http://www.nla.gov.au/services/CIP.html>
Genealogical standards and guidelines:
Published online by National Genealogical Society (US) on research,
citation, notekeeping, using record repositories, sharing information,
publishing, self improvement and using technology:
<http://www.ngsgenealogy.org/>
International Standard Book Number (ISBN) (Australia):
ISBN Agency
Bldg C3, 85 Turner Street (Locked Bag 20)
Port Melbourne VIC 3207
Australia
Phone: (03) 8645 0385
Fax: (03) 8645 0393
Email: isbn@thorpe.com.au
<http://www.thorpe.com.au>
ISBN (USA): <http://www.isbn.org/standards/home/index.asp>
Legal depostis and lending rights:
Legal Deposit (Australia): <http://www.nla.gov.au/services/ldeposit.html>
Legal Deposit (USA): <http://www.copyright.gov/circs/circ1.html#mdw>

Lending Right (PLR & ELR) Schemes (Australia):
   <http://www.dcita.gov.au/arts/arts/lending_schemes>
PLR (Canada): <http://www.plr-dpp.ca/>
PLR (New Zealand): <http://www.creativenz.govt.nz/>
PLR (UK): <http://www.plr.uk.com/textindex.htm>
The (US) Genealogical Proof Standard:
   <http://ourworld.compuserve.com/homepages/jkonvalinka/GPS.htm>

Websites on writing, publishing and word usage

Writing Centres

ACT Writers' Centre: <www.actwriters.org.au>
Australian Society of Authors: <www.asauthors.org>
New South Wales Writers' Centre: <http://www.nswwriterscentre.org.au/>
Northern Rivers Writers' Centre: <http://www.nrwc.org.au>
Northern Territory Writers' Centre: <http://www.ntwriters.com.au>
Queensland Writers Centre: <http://www.qwc.asn.au>
South Australian Writers' Centre: <http://www.sawriters.on.net>
Tasmanian Writers' Centre: <http://www.tasmanianwriters.org>
Victorian Writers' Centre: <http://www.writers-centre.org>
writingWA: <http://www.writerswritingwa.org>

Other websites

Dictionaries Online: <http://www.yourdictionary.com/>
Kansas University Writing Centre:
   <http://www.writing.ku.edu/students/guides.shtml>
Noeline Kyle's Writing Family History:
   <http://www.familyhistorywriting.bigpondhosting.com>
Purdue University online resources for writers:
   <http://owl.english.purdue.edu/>
UTS Centre for New Writing: <http://www.newwriting.uts.edu.au/>

Writelink—UK: <http://www.writelink.co.uk/>
Writing Links:

Writing awards, competitions and courses

The Association of Writers and Writing Programs:
<http://www.awpwriter.org/>
Australian Institute of Genealogical Studies: Alexander Henderson
Awards, President's Award and Manuscript Award (for Published
Family History)
Australian Institute of Genealogical Studies
PO Box 339
Blackburn VIC 3130
<http://www.aigs.org.au/ahaward.htm>
Department of Veterans' Affairs: The Story Writing and Art Competition
(SWAC), a popular annual event run specifically for members of
Victoria's ex-service community.
Story Writing and Art Competition
Department of Veterans' Affairs
GPO Box 87A
Melbourne VIC 3001
Email: Swac@dva.gov.au
<http://www.dva.gov.au/vic/services/swac/about.htm>
Family History Course (online and free): <http://www.ulladulla.info/fhc/>
FAW SAAB Community Writers' Award: An award for an anthology of
writing by a Writers' Club or Group.
PO Box 3036
Ripponlea VIC 3185
Phone: (03) 9528 7088
Fax: (03) 9528 7088
Email: niski@bigpond.com
<http://www.writers.asn.au/>
The FAW Walter Stone Memorial Award: A biennial competition for an
unpublished biography, monograph or bibliography not less than

5,000 words on some aspect of Australian literature.
<http://www.fawnsw.org.au/competitions.htm>
Fellowship of Australian Writers: Check this website for advertised
writing awards and competitions.
Fellowship of Australian Writers
PO Box 973
Eltham VIC 3095
Phone: (03) 9431 2370
<http://www.writers.asn.au/>
Greypath, free online course for seniors:
<http://www.greypath.com.au/courses/publishing/preamble.htm>
Janet Reakes Memorial Award: For an essay on family history. Entry
forms, closing date and terms of entry from:
AFTC Publishing Pty Limited
PO Box 322
Gosford NSW 2250
Australia
<http://www.aftc.com.au/JanetReakes/JRMA.html>
National Biography Award: For a published work of biographical or
autobiographical writing.
Mitchell Library Office
State Library of New South Wales
Macquarie Street
Sydney NSW 2000
Australia
<http://www.sl.nsw.gov.au/awards/biog.cfm>
National Genealogical Society Genealogical Writing Competitions: An
award for a specific, significant single contribution in the form of a
family genealogy or family history book published during the past
five years which serves to foster scholarship and/or otherwise
advances or promotes excellence in genealogy. A nomination form
is available online or by mail. Deadline for Submission—1 March
annually.
NGS Genealogical Writing Competitions
National Genealogical Society
3108 Columbia Pike, Suite 300
Arlington, Virginia 22204-4304 USA

Email: ngs@ngsgenealogy.org
<http://www.ngsgenealogy.org/comgenwritingfamily.cfm>
Nita Kibble Award: For women writers of a life-writing fiction or non-fiction book.
kibbleawards@perpetual.com.au
Phone: 1800 501 227
<http://www.perpetual.com.au/philanthropy/charitable_giving/charita ble_trusts.htm>
NSW Writers' Centre Book Prize for Best Self-Published Australian Book: NSW Writers Centre.
Phone: (02) 9555 9757
Email: nswwc@nswwriterscentre.org.au
<http://www.nswwriterscentre.org.au>
New South Wales Premier's Community and Regional History Prize: This prize ($15,000) is for a book, which makes a significant contribution to the understanding of Australian community, institutional or regional history. Inquiries and requests for nomination forms should be made to:
Program Support
NSW Ministry for the Arts
(Level 9, St James Centre, 111 Elizabeth Street, Sydney)
PO Box A226
Sydney South NSW 1235
Phone: (02) 9228 5533
Freecall: 1800 358 594 (within NSW)
Fax: (02) 9228 4722
Email: ministry@arts.nsw.gov.au
<http://www.arts.nsw.gov.au/awards/htm>
Queensland Family History Society Annual Family History Award:
Queensland Family History Society
PO Box 171
Indooroopilly Qld 4068
Email: fhaward@qfhs.org.au
<http://www.qfhs.org.au/FH_awards.htm>
Society of Australian Genealogists, Diploma in Family Historical Studies:
Society of Australian Genealogists
Richmond Villa

120 Kent Street
Sydney NSW 2000
Phone: (02) 9247 3953
Fax: (02) 9241 4872
Email: info@sag.org.au
<http://www.sag.org.au/services/diploma.htm>
Tasmanian Family History Society, Lillian Watson Family History Award:
The Award Coordinator
Lillian Watson Family History Award
PO Box 1290
Launceston TAS 7250
<http://www.tasfhs.org/award.htm>
Writing competitions overseas: <http://www.writelink.co.uk/>
Westfield/Waverley Library Award for Literature: Presented for a work
of literary fiction or non-fiction. The focus is on research and
writing with authors also required to submit a summary of the
research associated with the work. Enquiries and requests for
nomination forms should be addressed to:
The Project Officer
Westfield/Waverley Library Award for Literature
C/- Waverley Library
The Ron Lander Centre
32–48 Denison Street
Bondi Junction NSW 2022
Phone: (02) 9386 7709
Fax: (02) 9386 7700
Email: library_enquiries@waverley.nsw.gov.au
Guidelines and nomination forms can also be downloaded from:
<http://www.waverley.nsw.gov.au/library/award/>

Grants

Department of Defence, Army History Research Grants Scheme: Priority
is given to projects addressing military strategy and operations,

military social history and military heritage.
The Research Grants Officer
Army History Unit
CP4-2-031
Department of Defence
Canberra ACT 2600
Fax: (02) 6266 4044
Phone: (02) 6266 4248 (enquiries only)
(02) 6266 2744 (24 hr answering machine)
<http://www.defence.gov.au/army/ahu/grants/grants-index.htm>
Department of the Environment and Heritage, Sharing Australia's Stories
Grants Program: A program that gives all Australians the
opportunity to show how their stories have contributed to the great
events and themes that have shaped our nation. Grants between
$5,000 and $50,000 are available under the program. For more
information contact:
Department of the Environment and Heritage
GPO Box 787
Canberra ACT 2601
Phone: 1800 653 004
Fax: (02) 6274 2092
Email: storiesgrants@deh.gov.au
<http://www.deh.gov.au/heritage/programs/index.html#sharing>
Environment Australia, Grants to Voluntary Environment and Heritage
Organisations: Contact Details:
GVEHO Programme Team
Environment Australia
Phone: (02) 6274 2422
Fax: (02) 6274 1650
Email: gveho@ea.gov.au
<http://www.deh.gov.au/programs/gveho/index.htm>
Council Funding for heritage projects from local councils: The NSW
Heritage Office is prepared to support any rural council to establish
a local heritage fund at up to $8,000 dollar-for-dollar per year.
Grants are normally small but may be up to $10,000 per project
per year in special cases. Discuss with your local council heritage
officer if this is of interest to you. For further information contact:

NSW Heritage Office
Locked Bag 5020,
Parramatta NSW 2124
Phone: (02) 9873 8500
Fax: (02) 9873 8599
<http://www.heritage.nsw.gov.au/02_subnav_02.htm>
National Library of Australia—The Community Heritage Grants (CHG)
Program (apply through local family history or local history
organisation). The program provides grant funding of up to
$10,000 for preservation projects, and preservation and collection
management training through community-based workshops.
Community organisations such as historical societies, museums,
public libraries, archives, Indigenous and migrant community
groups which collect and provide public access to their cultural
heritage collections are eligible to apply:
The Coordinator
Community Heritage Grants
Public Programs Division
National Library of Australia
Parkes Place
Canberra ACT 2600
Phone: 02 6262 1147
Fax: 02 6273 4493
Email: chg@nla.gov.au
<http://www.nla.gov.au/chg/>
Northern Territory History Grants: Annual allocation of $50,000 in
individual grants ranging between $500 and $5,000. Grants are
allocated in July. Contact:
25 Cavenagh Street
Darwin NT 800
or
GPO Box 874
Darwin NT 801
Phone: (08) 8924 7677
Fax: (08) 8924 7660
<http://www.nt.gov.au/nta>

Parramatta City Heritage Program: Grants to Parramatta-based groups
for assistance towards cost of a Heritage Project. Contact:
30 Darcy Street
Parramatta NSW 2124
or
PO Box 32
Parramatta NSW 2124
Phone: (02) 9806 5112
Fax: (02) 9806 5914
<http://www.cultureandrecreation.gov.au/grants/program/10333-
4146.htm>
Public Record Office of Victoria, Local History Grants Program (LHGP):
This program aims to enable communities and individuals to
record, and publicly present, stories of notable events, movements
and people from Victoria's past. Contact:
Grants Program Information Victoria
Phone: 1300 366 356
or
Project Officer
Local History Grants Program
PO Box 2100
North Melbourne 3051
Email: daniel.wilksch@dvc.vic.gov.au
<http://www.prov.vic.gov.au/lhgp/welcome.asp>
Royal Australian Historical Society: The RAHS administers a Small
Grants program on behalf of the NSW Ministry for the Arts. These
grants provide support for projects, which assist the research and
publication of local history materials. For details concerning the
current guidelines, contact:
Manager
Outreach Programmes
Phone: (02) 9247 8001
Fax: (02) 9247 7854
Email: outreach@rahs.org.au
<http://www.rahs.org.au/grants.html>
South Australian History Fund: The South Australian History Fund
encourages and supports historical societies, museums, local councils

and other eligible community organisations to research, publish and preserve aspects of South Australia's social and community history. For general information about the Fund, please call:

The Community History Unit
Phone: (08) 8203 9888
<http://www.history.sa.gov.au/chu/programs/ch_fund.htm>

Writing festivals

Adelaide Writer's Week: <http://www.adelaidefestival.com.au/>
Australian Publishers & Authors Book Show NSW Writers' Centre:
    <http://www.nswwriterscentre.org.au>
Brisbane Writers Festival: <http://www.brisbanewritersfestival.com.au/>
Bryon Bay Writers Festival: <http://www.byronbaywritersfestival.com.au/>
Melbourne Writers Festival: <http://www.mwf.com.au/>
Overseas Writers Festivals: <http://www.author-
    network.com/festivals.html>
Sydney Writers Festival: <http://www.swf.org.au/>
Tasmanian Readers and Writer's Festival:
    <http://www.tasmanianwriters.org/>
Writing History Festival NSW Writers' Centre,
    <http://www.nswwriterscentre.org.au>

Published biography, autobiography, memoir and family history

Burcher, H.C., *Pioneers and their Better Halves or Seven Generations of Women in Australia*, Boolarong Publications, Brisbane, 1985
Bushell, A. (ed.), *Yesterday's Daughters: Stories of our past by women over 70*, Thomas Nelson Australia, Melbourne, 1986
Clarke, P., *A Colonial Woman: The life and times of Mary Braidwood Mowle*, Allen & Unwin, Sydney, 1986

Cordner, C., *A Mavis Singing: The Story of An Australian Family*, New South Wales University Press, Kensington, 1986

Cracknell, R., *Journey from Venice: A memoir*, Viking, Ringwood, 2000

Durack, M., *Kings in Grass Castles*, Constable and Co., London, 1959

Erickson, C., *The Girl from Botany Bay: The True Story of the Convict Mary Broad and her Extraordinary Escape*, Pan MacMillan, Melbourne, 2004

Falk, B., *No Other Home: An Anglo-Jewish Story 1833–1987*, Penguin Books, Ringwood, 1988

Facey, A.B., *A Fortunate Life*, Viking, Ringwood, 1984

Forster, M., *The Memory Box*, Penguin Books, London, 2000 (first published Chatto & Windus, 1999)

Frame, J., *An Angel at my Table*, Hutchinson Group, Auckland, 1984

Franklin, M., *Childhood at Brindabella: My first ten years*, Angus & Robertson, Sydney, 1974

Franklin, M., *My Brilliant Career*, Angus & Robertson, Sydney, 1979

Fry, C., *Can you find me: A family history*, Oxford University Press, Oxford/New York, 1978

Garner, H., *The Feel of Steel*, Picador/Pan Macmillan, Australia, 2001

Hackforth-Jones, P., *Barbara Baynton, between two worlds*, Penguin, Ringwood, 1989

Holmes, R., *Footsteps: Adventures of a Romantic Biographer*, Penguin Books, Ringwood, 1985

Horne, D., *The education of young Donald*, Penguin, Ringwood, 1988

Jefferies, B., *Three of a kind*, Sisters Publishing Ltd, Carlton, 1982

Ker Conway, J., *The Road from Coorain*, Alfred A. Knopf, New York, 1989

Killerby, C.K., *Ursula Frayne: A biography*, The University of Notre Dame Australia, an imprint of Fremantle Arts Centre Press, South Fremantle, 1996

Kyle, N., *Memories & Dreams: A Biography of Nurse Mary Kirkpatrick*, the author, Mullumbimby, 2001

Kyle, N., Semple, L. and Mulcahy, J. (eds), *Remembering Mothers: An inspiring anthology of short stories, letters and poetry*, Northern Rivers Family History Writers' Group, Alstonville, 2005

Lindsay, J., *Time Without Clocks*, Penguin Books, Middlesex, England, 1976

McCarthy, M., *Memories of a Catholic Girlhood*, Penguin Books, Middlesex, 1963

Mack, L., *Teens: A story of Australian schoolgirls*, Angus & Robertson, Sydney, 1897

McCourt, F., *Angela's Ashes: A Memoir*, HarperCollins, London, 1996

McCullagh, J., *Queensland Bound Too*, the author, Emerald, 2000

Magarey, S., *Unbridling the tongues of women: A biography of Catherine Helen Spence*, Hale & Iremonger, Sydney, 1985

Matthews, B., *Louisa*, McPhee Gribble/Penguin Books, Fitzroy/Ringwood, 1987

Modjeska, D., *Poppy*, McPhee Gribble, Ringwood, 1990

Morgan, S., *My Place*, Fremantle Arts Centre Press, Fremantle, 1987

Mulcahy, J. Gracie, *Other Than English*, Dragonwych Publishing, Goonellabah, 2006.

Norst, M.J., *Burnum Burnum: A warrior for peace*, Kangaroo Press, East Roseville, 1999

O'Faolin, N., *Are You Somebody?*, Sceptre Books, London, 1996

Painter, S., *The bean patch: A memoir*, Flamingo, Pymble, 2002

Park, R., *A Fence Around the Cuckoo*, Penguin Books, Ringwood, 1992

Peck, S., *All-American boy: A memoir*, Scribner, New York, 1995

Richardson, H. H. (pseud), *The Getting of Wisdom*, Heinemann, London, 1931 (first published 1910)

Scott, M., *Changing Countries: On moving from one island to another*, ABC Books, Sydney, 2000

Scott, M., *Family Album: A Novel of Secrets and Memories*, Vintage/Random House, Sydney, 2000.

Simson, D., *Caroline's Story: The story of the Miskin Family of Kent in Queensland*, the author, Brisbane, 1997

Stewart, M., *Autobiography of My Mother*, Penguin, Underwood, 1985

Tasma (Jessie Couvreur), *Uncle Piper of Piper's Hill*, Trübner, London, 1892

Tisdall, C., *Forerunners: The Saga of a Family of Teachers*, Graham Publications, Walhalla, 1961

White, P., *Flaws in the Glass: A self-portrait*, Penguin Books, Ringwood, 1988

Appendix ᥰ

GENEALOGICAL
SOFTWARE PROGRAMS

R ecent versions of Ancestral Quest, Family
Tree Legends, GenBox, Roots Magic,
Family Tree Maker, Personal Ancestral File,
Legacy, The Master Genealogist and others have the
functionality to construct a table of contents, index, endnotes,
footnotes and export these to your word-processing program.
The most recent versions also promise to print out some form
of book.

Keep in mind, however, the old adage—rubbish in, rubbish
out! A genealogy software program is a database program,
albeit an increasingly sophisticated one. Its major function is
to allow users to enter large amounts of data and facilitate
the printing of charts and reports. These charts and reports
can then constitute the basis of a book.

Genalogy software programs can help you put together a
simple, basic book. Most of the book features in genealogical

software programs generally have pre-designed formats associated with the reports facility. All of the genealogical programs appear to have based their book function on collating together a title page, contents page, narratives, individual, generation and/or other reports plus an index, in a logical sequence. You can then print this collection of pages into a book.

Some programs also allow you to insert and edit photographs, make a scrapbook, insert sound, construct a video and publish to the web. The free and standard versions of some software have fewer book-making features.

The following websites are useful for comparing recent releases of genealogy software:

Louis Kessler's Genealogy Software Links: <http://www.lkessler.com/gplinks.shtml>

Richard Wilson's Comparison of Genealogy Software Programs: <http://www.familychronicle.com/software.html>

See also the website, About Desktop Publishing, on writing and publishing from genealogical software <http://desktoppub.about.com/library/weekly/aa011502b.htm>

Family Tree Legends has an internal book-assembly function and it is easy to use with a Books option on a pulldown menu. Within the Legends pre-formatted menus you can add individual reports including ancestors and descendants, family group sheets, kinship reports, pedigrees and a timeline.

The Books function also allows for the addition of addresses, alternate facts, census data, LDS ordinance reports, military information, places, sources and other customised data. The user is able to add or remove information, move items around and edit the format and text very quickly on the easy-to-use menu. Family Tree Legends also allows you to publish your data to the web with little effort on your part. Legends has an attractive and useful way of constructing, printing and publishing a book. You can also preview the book and print it from the Books Option.

The standard edition of Legacy has many functions to help with constructing a book, located under the Report menu. There are four options beginning with the Ancestor Book option—a book-style report moving *backwards* through the generations, based on the German Abnentafel (ancestor table). The Descendant Book option moves *forward* from the individual for a given number of generations and can be done in Modified Register or Register format. (The Modified Register format describes each person in a narrative format and assigns each person a number. The Register format is similar but only individuals with children are assigned a number.) The Descendant Narrative Book option is a book-style report that begins with a specific person and moves forward through descendants for a given number of generations. It is similar to the Modified Register Descendant Book but more abbreviated.

Progeny Software's Legacy Charting Companion add-on can be used to add fancy colour and additional formats to your chart section in Legacy. Legacy is Gedcom compatible and you can publish to a website. A basic version of Legacy is free to download at: <http://www.legacyfamilytree.com./>.

The Master Genealogist (TMG) requires effort from a beginner to learn all of the functions and become proficient in their use. You can expect to spend some time reading the manual to master TMG and also to work out how the book functions can aid your book printing and publishing. Nonetheless, this is an impressive program and your persistence and effort will be rewarded. It is one of the best software programs available for organising and managing large amounts of data and a plethora of files.

TMG can do most of the functions required to make a book without the need for Progeny add-on software. You can add an index, edit as you go with a word processor (such as Word), insert photographs and reformat at any time. Pagination, footnotes and additional columns are all possible. TMG can tailor wording, dates and places for events such as immigratin or land purchase.

Once you become familiar with any program you can experiment and expand your usage. Put in some hours of research on which program might be best suited to your needs, peruse the websites cited above and test drive some of the free versions before making a decision to purchase.

INDEX